maranGraphics'™
Simplified Computer Guide

Microsoft® Excel 4.0 for Windows™

Ruth Maran

maranGraphics Inc.

Mississauga, Ontario, Canada

Distributed in United States
by Regents/Prentice Hall

Telephone: 1-800-223-1360
Fax: 1-800-445-6991

Distributed in Canada
by Prentice Hall Canada

Telephone: 1-800-567-3800
Fax: 416-299-2529

Distributed Internationally
by Simon & Schuster

Telephone: 201-767-4990
Fax: 201-767-5625

maranGraphics'™ *Simplified Computer Guide*
Microsoft ® Excel 4.0 for Windows™

Copyright©   maranGraphics Inc., 1992
              5755 Coopers Avenue
              Mississauga, Ontario, Canada
              L4Z 1R9

              Screen shots ©1987-1991 Microsoft
              Corporation. Reprinted with permission
              from Microsoft Corporation.

Published 1992.

Canadian Cataloguing in Publication Data

Maran, Ruth
    MaranGraphics' simplified computer guide,
Microsoft Excel 4.0 for Windows

Includes index.

1. Microsoft Excel (Computer program).   2. Microsoft
Excel 4 for Windows.   3. Business - Computer programs.
4. WINDOWS (Computer program).   I. Title.

HF5548.4.M523M52 1992 650'.0285'5369 C92-094769-7

Acknowledgements

Special thanks to Victor Pitchkur of Microsoft Canada
Inc., and to Saverio C. Tropiano, B.Sc., B.A. for their
support and consultation.

To the dedicated staff at maranGraphics Inc. and
HyperImage Inc., including Monica DeVries,
Jim C. Leung, Jill Maran, Judy Maran, Robert Maran,
David Ross and Gavin Yong for their contributions.

To Eric Feistmantl who was always there to solve my
technical and operational problems.

To Maxine Maran for providing the organizational skill
to keep the project under control.

And finally, a special appreciation to Richard Maran
who originated the easy-to-use graphic format of this
guide. Thank you for your inspiration and guidance.

Trademark Acknowledgements

Microsoft, MS and MS-DOS,
are registered trademarks
of Microsoft Corporation.

Autosum, the Microsoft
Mouse design, and
Windows are trademarks of
Microsoft Corporation.

HP, Hewlett-Packard,
LaserJet and DeskJet are
registered trademarks of
Hewlett-Packard Company.

Q+E is a trademark of
Pioneer Software Systems
Corporation.

**Cover Design &
Graphics Consultant:**
Jim C. Leung

Art Director:
Jim C. Leung

Production:
Monica DeVries
Jim C. Leung
David Ross

Linotronic L-330 Output:
HyperImage Inc.

Table of Contents

READ ME FIRST

Microsoft® Excel 4.0 for Windows™ is a spreadsheet package used to create documents that help you organize, analyze, and perform calculations on your data.

maranGraphics uses a unique two-page format, as illustrated to the right.

The screen-by-screen method displays exactly what you see on screen as you move through the program.

All chapters in this guide are listed on the right side of each two-page format. The current chapter is highlighted in red type.

All topics within the current chapter are displayed on the top right of each two-page format. The current topic is highlighted in red type.

Think of it as being in a shopping mall, using a "You Are Here" display to find a particular store.

Typical Two-Page Format

CREATE A CHART

The ChartWizard leads you through five steps to create a chart using data from your worksheet.

In this example, the **Revenue and Total Expenses for the months of Jan, Feb, and Mar will be charted.**

Data Range to be Charted (Step 1 of 5)

1 Select the column headings you want to chart (example: **A3** to **D3**).

2 Press and hold down the **Ctrl** key as you select the other rows you want to chart (example: **A5** to **D5**, then **A10** to **D10**).

3 Release the mouse button, then the **Ctrl** key.

4 Click the **ChartWizard** tool and the mouse pointer changes to **+**.

Chart Type (Step 2 of 5)

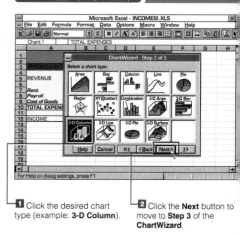

1 Click the desired chart type (example: **3-D Column**).

2 Click the **Next** button to move to **Step 3** of the **ChartWizard**.

All topics within the current chapter are displayed. The current topic is highlighted in red type.

CREATE A CHART	MOVE A CHART	RESIZE A CHART	CHANGE CHART DATA	CHANGE CHART TYPE OR FORMAT	ROTATE A CHART

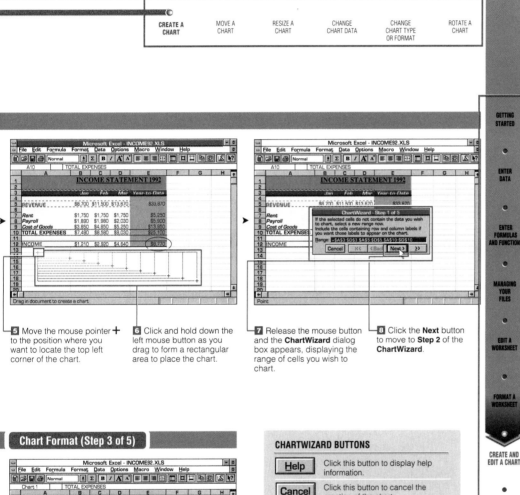

5 Move the mouse pointer **+** to the position where you want to locate the top left corner of the chart.

6 Click and hold down the left mouse button as you drag to form a rectangular area to place the chart.

7 Release the mouse button and the **ChartWizard** dialog box appears, displaying the range of cells you wish to chart.

8 Click the **Next** button to move to **Step 2** of the **ChartWizard**.

All chapters in the guide are displayed. The current chapter is highlighted in red type.

Chart Format (Step 3 of 5)

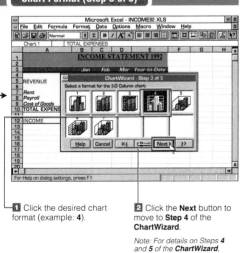

1 Click the desired chart format (example: **4**).

2 Click the **Next** button to move to **Step 4** of the **ChartWizard**.

Note: For details on Steps 4 and 5 of the ChartWizard, refer to page 68.

CHARTWIZARD BUTTONS

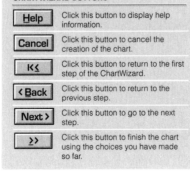

Help	Click this button to display help information.
Cancel	Click this button to cancel the creation of the chart.
K<	Click this button to return to the first step of the ChartWizard.
< Back	Click this button to return to the previous step.
Next >	Click this button to go to the next step.
>>	Click this button to finish the chart using the choices you have made so far.

START MICROSOFT EXCEL

Start Microsoft Excel

`C:\>win_`

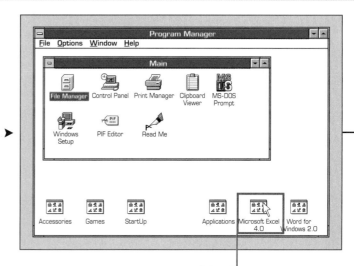

1 To start Microsoft® Excel from MS-DOS, type **win**. Then press **Enter**.

■ The **Program Manager** window is displayed.

All your programs (example: **Word for Windows 2.0**, **Microsoft Excel 4.0**) are started from the Program Manager.

2 To open the **Microsoft Excel 4.0** group icon, move the mouse pointer over its icon and click the left button twice in quick succession.

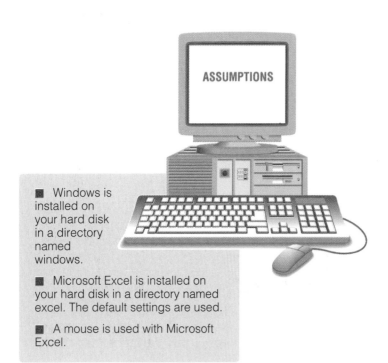

ASSUMPTIONS

■ Windows is installed on your hard disk in a directory named windows.

■ Microsoft Excel is installed on your hard disk in a directory named excel. The default settings are used.

■ A mouse is used with Microsoft Excel.

START
MICROSOFT
EXCEL

MAXIMIZE AND
RESTORE A
WINDOW

EXIT
MICROSOFT
EXCEL

HELP

SELECT
CELLS

MOVING
THROUGH A
WORKSHEET

GETTING
STARTED

● ENTER
DATA

● ENTER
FORMULAS
AND FUNCTIONS

● MANAGING
YOUR
FILES

● EDIT A
WORKSHEET

● FORMAT A
WORKSHEET

● CREATE AND
EDIT A CHART

● PRINT

● OUTLINE A
WORKSHEET

● CREATE AND
USE A
DATABASE

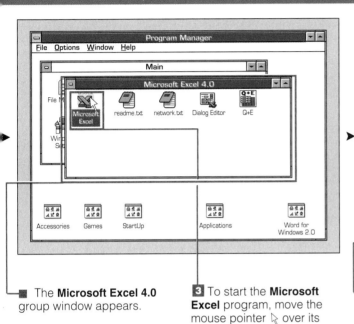

■ The **Microsoft Excel 4.0** group window appears.

3 To start the **Microsoft Excel** program, move the mouse pointer ⍩ over its icon and click the left button twice in quick succession.

■ Microsoft Excel opens up a new worksheet called **Sheet1**.

■ This worksheet window is also called a document. The name of the document can be renamed when you save it to your hard disk.

ACTIVE CELL
Data or formulas are entered into the active cell.

COLUMN
The worksheet contains 256 columns.

ROW
The worksheet contains 16,384 rows.

CELL
A cell is defined by the intersection of a row and column.

The **readme.txt** file contains the latest revisions and notes for Microsoft Excel.

readme.txt

The **network.txt** file contains information on using Microsoft Excel in a network environment.

network.txt

The **Dialog Editor** is used to create custom dialog boxes for macros.

Dialog Editor

Q+E is a database program that can manipulate and update database files from an assortment of database systems.

Q+E

Note: These readme files and programs are for advanced users. Refer to your Microsoft Excel User's Guide for more information.

USING THE KEYBOARD

If key names are separated by a plus sign (+), press and hold down the first key before pressing the second key (example: **Shift+Tab**).

If key names are separated by a comma (,), press and release the first key before pressing the second key (example: **Alt,F**).

USING THE MOUSE

For this guide, the following shortcuts are used:

■ "Move the mouse pointer ⍩ over **xx** and click the left button" becomes:

Click xx

■ "Move the mouse pointer ⍩ over **xx** and click the left button twice in quick succession" becomes:

Double click xx

Maximize a Window

Restore a Window

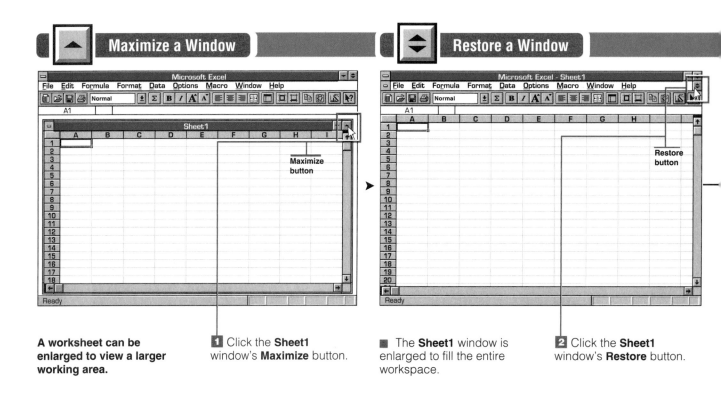

A worksheet can be enlarged to view a larger working area.

1 Click the **Sheet1** window's **Maximize** button.

■ The **Sheet1** window is enlarged to fill the entire workspace.

2 Click the **Sheet1** window's **Restore** button.

Exit Microsoft Excel

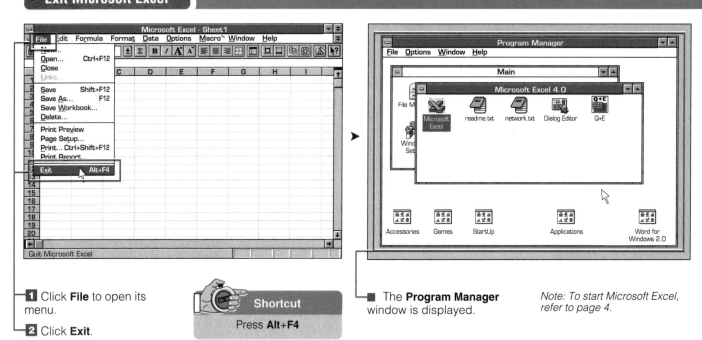

1 Click **File** to open its menu.

2 Click **Exit**.

Shortcut

Press **Alt+F4**

■ The **Program Manager** window is displayed.

Note: To start Microsoft Excel, refer to page 4.

START
MICROSOFT
EXCEL

**MAXIMIZE AND
RESTORE A
WINDOW**

**EXIT
MICROSOFT
EXCEL**

HELP

SELECT
CELLS

MOVING
THROUGH A
WORKSHEET

GETTING
STARTED

●

ENTER
DATA

●

ENTER
FORMULAS
AND FUNCTIONS

●

MANAGING
YOUR
FILES

●

EDIT A
WORKSHEET

●

FORMAT A
WORKSHEET

●

CREATE AND
EDIT A CHART

●

PRINT

●

OUTLINE A
WORKSHEET

●

CREATE AND
USE A
DATABASE

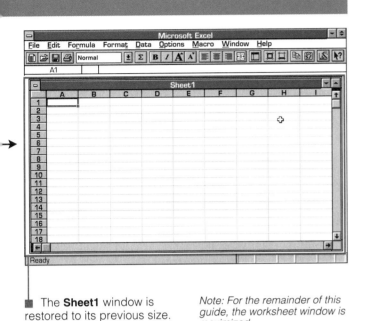

■ The **Sheet1** window is restored to its previous size.

Note: For the remainder of this guide, the worksheet window is maximized.

KEYBOARD SHORTCUT TO SELECT MENU COMMANDS

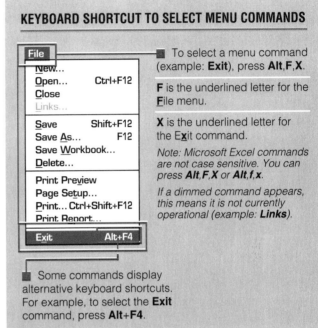

■ To select a menu command (example: **Exit**), press **Alt,F,X**.

F is the underlined letter for the **F**ile menu.

X is the underlined letter for the E**x**it command.

*Note: Microsoft Excel commands are not case sensitive. You can press **Alt,F,X** or **Alt,f,x**.*

*If a dimmed command appears, this means it is not currently operational (example: **Links**).*

■ Some commands display alternative keyboard shortcuts. For example, to select the **Exit** command, press **Alt+F4**.

If this dialog box appears when trying to exit Microsoft Excel, you have not saved changes you made to the worksheet.

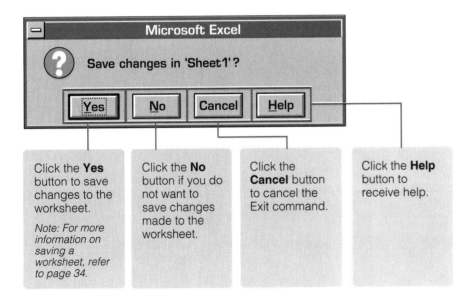

Click the **Yes** button to save changes to the worksheet.

Note: For more information on saving a worksheet, refer to page 34.

Click the **No** button if you do not want to save changes made to the worksheet.

Click the **Cancel** button to cancel the Exit command.

Click the **Help** button to receive help.

HELP

Context Sensitive Help

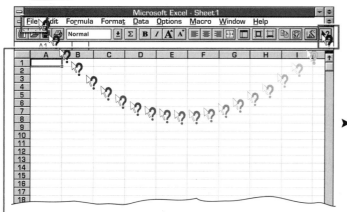

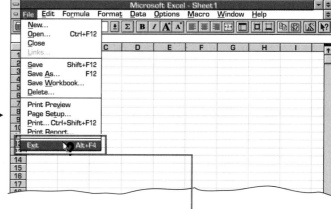

This feature permits you to receive help information for any item on the screen by clicking that item.

1 Click the **Help** tool and the mouse pointer ⌖ changes to ⌖**?**.

2 To receive help on a menu command, click a menu title (example: **File**) to open its menu.

■ The File menu is opened.

3 Click the command (example: **Exit**) you want help on.

Help Contents

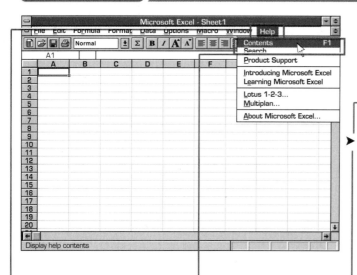

Help Contents displays a list of the main Help topics.

1 Click **Help** to open its menu.

2 Click **Contents** and the **Microsoft Excel Help** window appears.

3 Move the mouse pointer ⌖ over a topic you want information on (example: **Basic Concepts**), and it turns into ⍟. Then click the left mouse button.

Note: This only applies to underlined text.

START
MICROSOFT
EXCEL

MAXIMIZE AND
RESTORE A
WINDOW

EXIT
MICROSOFT
EXCEL

HELP

SELECT
CELLS

MOVING
THROUGH A
WORKSHEET

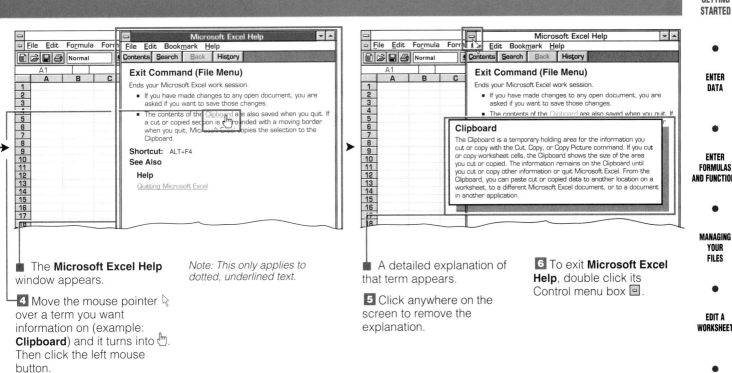

■ The **Microsoft Excel Help** window appears.

Note: This only applies to dotted, underlined text.

4 Move the mouse pointer ⌖ over a term you want information on (example: **Clipboard**) and it turns into ⌐. Then click the left mouse button.

■ A detailed explanation of that term appears.

5 Click anywhere on the screen to remove the explanation.

6 To exit **Microsoft Excel Help**, double click its Control menu box ⊟.

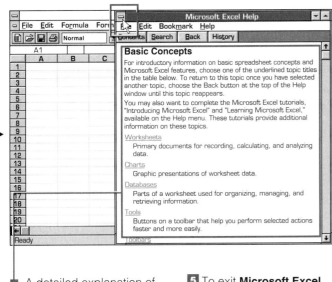

■ A detailed explanation of that topic appears.

4 Move the mouse pointer ⌖ over the next topic of interest and it turns into ⌐. Then click the left mouse button.

5 To exit **Microsoft Excel Help**, double click its Control menu box ⊟.

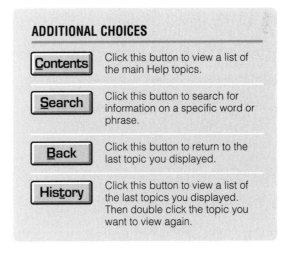

ADDITIONAL CHOICES

Contents Click this button to view a list of the main Help topics.

Search Click this button to search for information on a specific word or phrase.

Back Click this button to return to the last topic you displayed.

History Click this button to view a list of the last topics you displayed. Then double click the topic you want to view again.

GETTING
STARTED

●
ENTER
DATA

●
ENTER
FORMULAS
AND FUNCTIONS

●
MANAGING
YOUR
FILES

●
EDIT A
WORKSHEET

●
FORMAT A
WORKSHEET

●
CREATE AND
EDIT A CHART

●
PRINT

●
OUTLINE A
WORKSHEET

●
CREATE AND
USE A
DATABASE

SELECT CELLS

Select a Cell

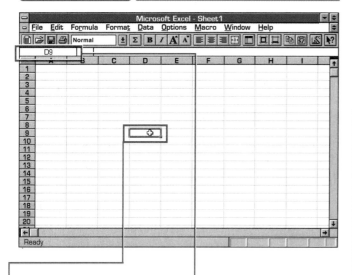

1 Click the cell (example: **D9**) you want to select.

■ The cell becomes the active cell and displays a dark border.

■ The Reference area displays the location (column and row) of the active cell.

Select a Row

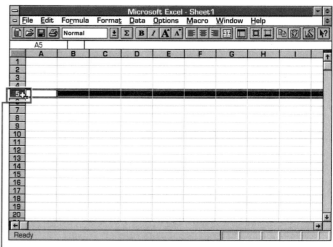

1 To select a row, click the row heading (example: **5**).

Note: To cancel the selection, click anywhere on the worksheet.

Select a Cell Range

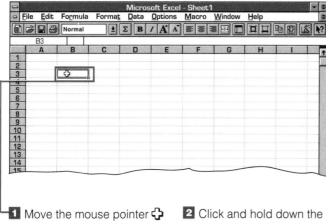

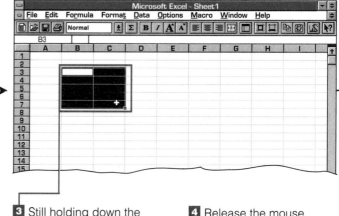

1 Move the mouse pointer ✛ over the first cell of the range (example: **B3**) you want to select.

2 Click and hold down the left mouse button.

3 Still holding down the button, drag the mouse to select the cell range.

4 Release the mouse button.

Note: To cancel the selection, click anywhere on the worksheet.

START
MICROSOFT
EXCEL

MAXIMIZE AND
RESTORE A
WINDOW

EXIT
MICROSOFT
EXCEL

HELP

**SELECT
CELLS**

MOVING
THROUGH A
WORKSHEET

GETTING
STARTED

ENTER
DATA

ENTER
FORMULAS
AND FUNCTIONS

MANAGING
YOUR
FILES

EDIT A
WORKSHEET

FORMAT A
WORKSHEET

CREATE AND
EDIT A CHART

PRINT

OUTLINE A
WORKSHEET

CREATE AND
USE A
DATABASE

Select a Column

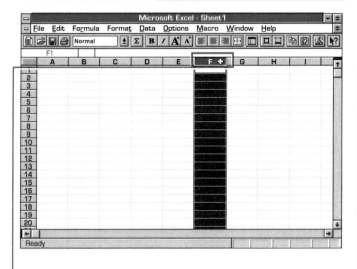

1 To select a column, click the column heading (example: **F**).

Note: To cancel the selection, click anywhere on the worksheet.

Select the Entire Worksheet

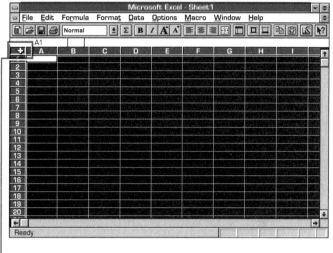

1 To select the entire worksheet, click the **Select All** button.

Note: To cancel the selection, click anywhere on the worksheet.

Select Two Cell Ranges

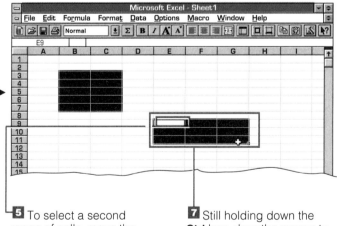

5 To select a second range of cells, move the mouse pointer ✚ over the first cell of the range (example: **E9**) you want to select.

6 Press and hold down the **Ctrl** key.

7 Still holding down the **Ctrl** key, drag the mouse to select the second cell range.

8 Release the **Ctrl** key, then release the mouse button.

*Note: To select more than two cell ranges, repeat steps **5** to **8**.*

IMPORTANT

You must select the cells you want to work with before executing most Microsoft Excel commands.

11

MOVING THROUGH A WORKSHEET

Using the Keyboard

MOVE ONE CELL IN ANY DIRECTION

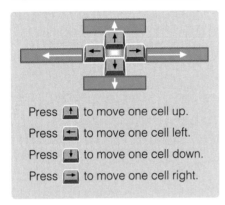

Press ⬆ to move one cell up.

Press ⬅ to move one cell left.

Press ⬇ to move one cell down.

Press ➡ to move one cell right.

MOVE TO CELL A1

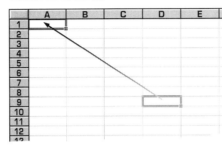

Press **Ctrl+Home** to move to cell **A1** from anywhere in the worksheet.

MOVE ONE SCREEN UP OR DOWN

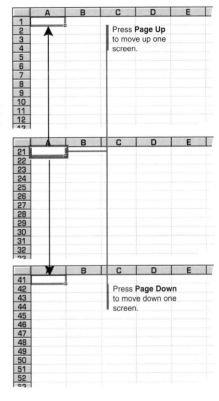

Press **Page Up** to move up one screen.

Press **Page Down** to move down one screen.

Note: Press **Ctrl+Page Down** to move one screen to the right. Press **Ctrl+Page Up** to move one screen to the left.

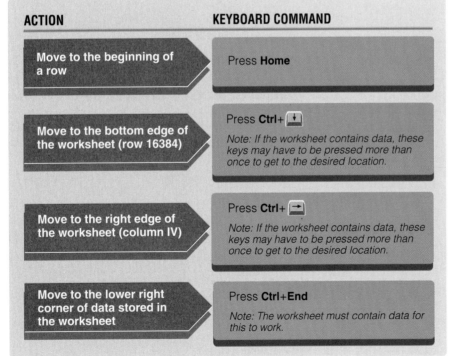

ACTION	KEYBOARD COMMAND
Move to the beginning of a row	Press **Home**
Move to the bottom edge of the worksheet (row 16384)	Press **Ctrl+ ⬇** Note: If the worksheet contains data, these keys may have to be pressed more than once to get to the desired location.
Move to the right edge of the worksheet (column IV)	Press **Ctrl+ ➡** Note: If the worksheet contains data, these keys may have to be pressed more than once to get to the desired location.
Move to the lower right corner of data stored in the worksheet	Press **Ctrl+End** Note: The worksheet must contain data for this to work.

NUM LOCK

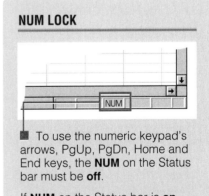

■ To use the numeric keypad's arrows, PgUp, PgDn, Home and End keys, the **NUM** on the Status bar must be **off**.

If **NUM** on the Status bar is **on**, press 🔲 to turn it off.

START
MICROSOFT
EXCEL

MAXIMIZE AND
RESTORE A
WINDOW

EXIT
MICROSOFT
EXCEL

HELP

SELECT
CELLS

**MOVING
THROUGH A
WORKSHEET**

 Using the Mouse

GETTING
STARTED

•

ENTER
DATA

•

ENTER
FORMULAS
AND FUNCTIONS

•

MANAGING
YOUR
FILES

•

EDIT A
WORKSHEET

•

FORMAT A
WORKSHEET

•

CREATE AND
EDIT A CHART

•

PRINT

•

OUTLINE A
WORKSHEET

•

CREATE AND
USE A
DATABASE

SCROLL UP OR DOWN

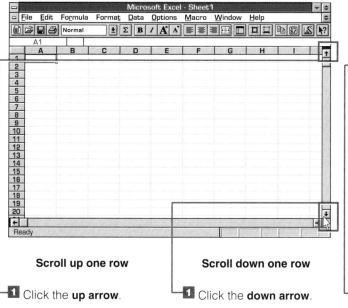

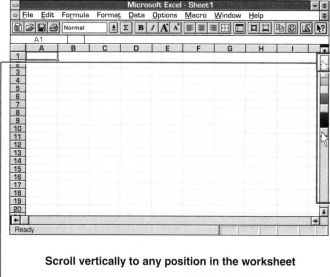

Scroll up one row

1 Click the **up arrow**.

Scroll down one row

1 Click the **down arrow**.

Scroll vertically to any position in the worksheet

1 Move the mouse pointer over the **Scroll box**. Click the left button and hold it down.

2 To move proportionally down the worksheet, drag the **Scroll box** proportionally (example: **halfway**) down the Scroll bar. Then release the button.

SCROLL LEFT OR RIGHT

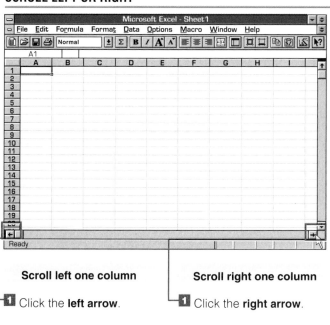

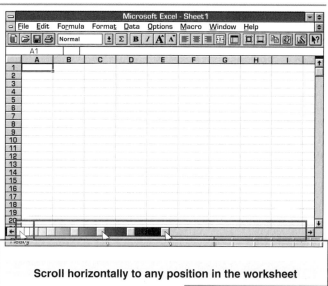

Scroll left one column

1 Click the **left arrow**.

Scroll right one column

1 Click the **right arrow**.

Scroll horizontally to any position in the worksheet

1 Move the mouse pointer over the **Scroll box**. Click the left button and hold it down.

2 To move proportionally across the worksheet, drag the **Scroll box** proportionally (example: **halfway**) along the Scroll bar. Then release the button.

ENTER TEXT   ENTER NUMBERS

☑ Enter Text

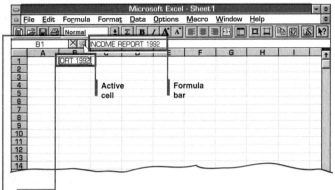

Active cell

Formula bar

1 Click the cell you want to enter text into (example: **B1**).

2 Type the text (example: **INCOME REPORT 1992**). As you type, the text appears in the active cell and in the formula bar.

*Note: If you make a mistake typing, press **Backspace** and retype.*

3 Click the Enter ☑ box, or press **Enter** to place the text in the cell.

*Note: To cancel the entry, click the Cancel ☒ box, or press **Esc**.*

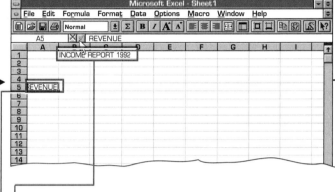

■ The text is entered into the cell.

4 Click the next cell you want to enter text into (example: **A5**).

5 Type the text (example: **REVENUE**).

6 Click the Enter ☑ box, or press **Enter** to place the text in the cell.

*Note: To cancel the entry, click the Cancel ☒ box, or press **Esc**.*

☑ Enter Numbers

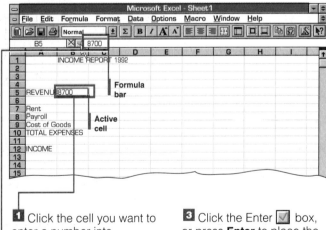

Formula bar

Active cell

1 Click the cell you want to enter a number into (example: **B5**).

2 Type the number (example: **8700**). As you type, the number appears in the active cell and in the formula bar.

*Note: If you make a mistake typing, press **Backspace** and retype.*

3 Click the Enter ☑ box, or press **Enter** to place the number in the cell.

*Note: To cancel the entry, click the Cancel ☒ box, or press **Esc**.*

■ The number is entered into the cell.

4 Click the next cell you want to enter a number into (example: **C5**).

5 Type the number (example: **11500**).

6 Click the Enter ☑ box, or press **Enter** to place the number in the cell.

*Note: To cancel the entry, click the Cancel ☒ box, or press **Esc**.*

| ENTER TEXT | ENTER NUMBERS | EDIT DATA | UNDO | AUTOFILL TEXT | AUTOFILL THE SAME DATA | AUTOFILL NUMBERS | DELETE DATA |

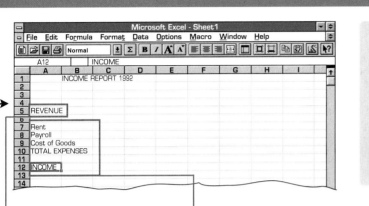

LONG TEXT

■ If text is too long to fit in a cell, it spills over into the adjacent cell(s) if it is empty.

■ If the adjacent cell already contains data, Microsoft Excel displays as much of the text as the column width will allow. To display all text, the column must be widened (refer to page 42).

■ The text is entered into the cell.

7 Type and enter the remaining text by repeating steps **1** to **3** for each text entry.

Shortcut

Press →, ←, ↓ or ↑ to enter text and move to the next cell.

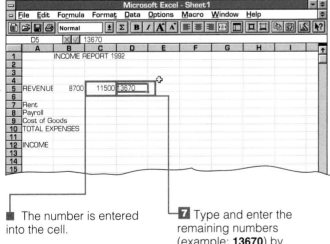

LONG NUMBERS

■ If a number is too long to fit in a cell, Microsoft Excel tries to display it exponentially.

■ If the exponential form is still too long, number signs (###) are displayed in the cell. To display the entire number, the column must be widened (refer to page 42).

■ The number is entered into the cell.

7 Type and enter the remaining numbers (example: **13670**) by repeating steps **1** to **3** for each number you want to enter.

*Note: If you begin a number with a plus sign **+**, the sign is ignored.*

*To enter a negative number, begin it with a minus sign – (example: **–13670**).*

Shortcut

Press →, ←, ↓ or ↑ to enter a number and move to the next cell.

GETTING STARTED

ENTER DATA

ENTER FORMULAS AND FUNCTIONS

MANAGING YOUR FILES

EDIT A WORKSHEET

FORMAT A WORKSHEET

CREATE AND EDIT A CHART

PRINT

OUTLINE A WORKSHEET

CREATE AND USE A DATABASE

15

EDIT DATA

UNDO

Edit Data

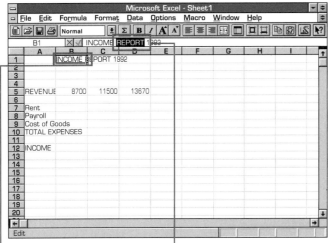

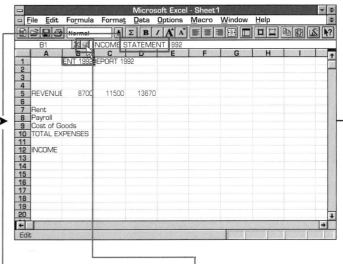

1 Click the cell that contains the data you want to change (example: **B1**).

2 In the formula bar, click and hold down the left mouse button as you drag over the character(s) you want to replace (example: **REPORT**). Then release the button.

3 Type the correction (example: **STATEMENT**).

*Note: If you make a mistake typing, press **Backspace** and retype.*

4 Click the Enter ☑ box, or press **Enter**.

Undo

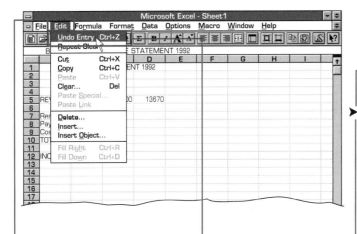

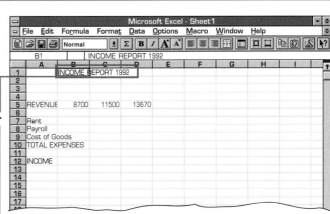

Undo cancels your last entry or command. This only works immediately after performing an action.

1 Click **Edit** and its menu appears.

2 Click **Undo Entry**.

*Note: The **Undo** command listed in the Edit menu displays the last command or action you performed.*

Can't Undo *appears in the Edit menu if you cannot undo your last action.*

■ Your last entry or command is cancelled (example: **STATEMENT** is changed back to **REPORT**).

Shortcut

Press **Ctrl+Z**

ENTER
TEXT

ENTER
NUMBERS

**EDIT
DATA**

UNDO

AUTOFILL
TEXT

AUTOFILL
THE SAME
DATA

AUTOFILL
NUMBERS

DELETE
DATA

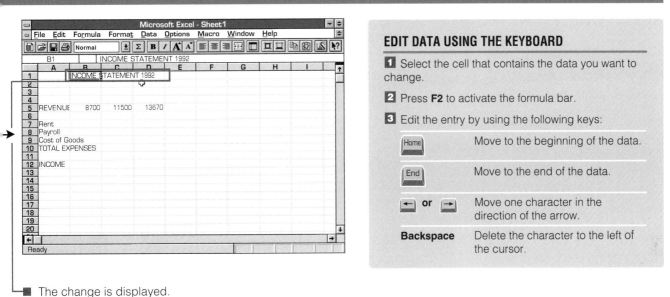

EDIT DATA USING THE KEYBOARD

1 Select the cell that contains the data you want to change.

2 Press **F2** to activate the formula bar.

3 Edit the entry by using the following keys:

Home	Move to the beginning of the data.
End	Move to the end of the data.
← or →	Move one character in the direction of the arrow.
Backspace	Delete the character to the left of the cursor.

■ The change is displayed.

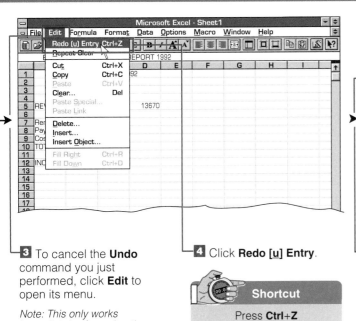

3 To cancel the **Undo** command you just performed, click **Edit** to open its menu.

*Note: This only works immediately after using the **Undo** command.*

4 Click **Redo [u] Entry**.

Shortcut

Press **Ctrl+Z**

■ The last **Undo** command you performed is reversed (example: **REPORT** is changed back to **STATEMENT**).

GETTING
STARTED

ENTER
DATA

ENTER
FORMULAS
AND FUNCTIONS

MANAGING
YOUR
FILES

EDIT A
WORKSHEET

FORMAT A
WORKSHEET

CREATE AND
EDIT A CHART

PRINT

OUTLINE A
WORKSHEET

CREATE AND
USE A
DATABASE

AUTOFILL TEXT

AUTOFILL THE SAME DATA

➕ AutoFill Text

By using the AutoFill feature, Microsoft Excel can automatically enter a series into your worksheet. Examples are displayed below:

Starting Text	AutoFill Text		
Jan	Feb	Mar	Apr
Qtr 1	Qtr 2	Qtr 3	Qtr 4
Mon	Tue	Wed	Thu
Product 1	Product 2	Product 3	Product 4
2nd Term	3rd Term	4th Term	5th Term

Note: The AutoFill feature works in both the horizontal and vertical directions.

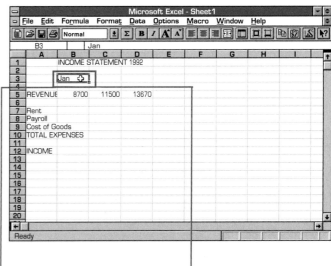

1 Click the cell (example: **B3**) you want to contain the first series entry.

2 Type and enter the text (example: **Jan**) you want to begin the series. Then click the cell (example: **B3**) to select it.

➕ AutoFill the Same Data

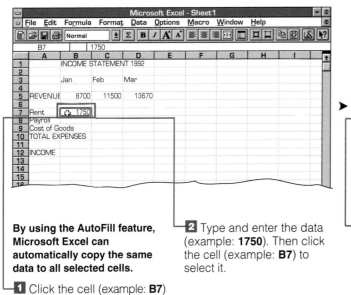

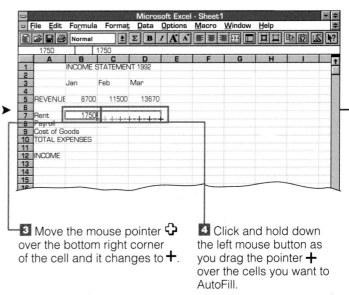

By using the AutoFill feature, Microsoft Excel can automatically copy the same data to all selected cells.

1 Click the cell (example: **B7**) you want to contain the data to be copied.

2 Type and enter the data (example: **1750**). Then click the cell (example: **B7**) to select it.

3 Move the mouse pointer ⟐ over the bottom right corner of the cell and it changes to ➕.

4 Click and hold down the left mouse button as you drag the pointer ➕ over the cells you want to AutoFill.

ENTER
TEXT

ENTER
NUMBERS

EDIT
DATA

UNDO

**AUTOFILL
TEXT**

**AUTOFILL
THE SAME
DATA**

AUTOFILL
NUMBERS

DELETE
DATA

GETTING
STARTED

ENTER
DATA

ENTER
FORMULAS
AND FUNCTIONS

MANAGING
YOUR
FILES

EDIT A
WORKSHEET

FORMAT A
WORKSHEET

CREATE AND
EDIT A CHART

PRINT

OUTLINE A
WORKSHEET

CREATE AND
USE A
DATABASE

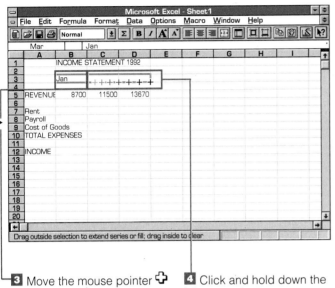

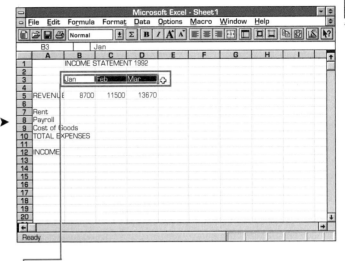

3 Move the mouse pointer ✛ over the bottom right corner of the cell (example: **B3**) and it changes to ✛.

4 Click and hold down the left mouse button as you drag the pointer ✛ over the cells you want to AutoFill.

5 Release the mouse button, and the series (example: **Feb**, **Mar**) is added to your worksheet.

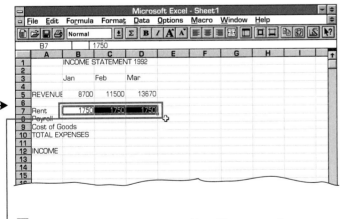

5 Release the mouse button, and the data is copied to all selected cells.

Note: You can use the same method to copy text.

AUTOFILL NUMBERS   DELETE DATA

➕ AutoFill Numbers

By using the AutoFill feature, Microsoft Excel can automatically enter a series of numbers into your worksheet. Examples are displayed below:

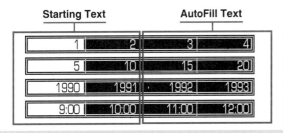

Starting Text		AutoFill Text	
1	2	3	4
5	10	15	20
1990	1991	1992	1993
9:00	10:00	11:00	12:00

Note: The AutoFill feature works in both the horizontal and vertical directions.

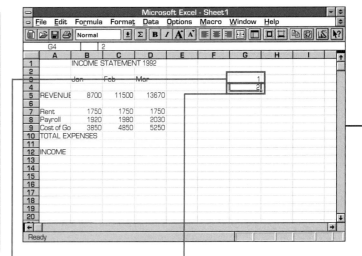

1 Click the cell (example: **G3**) you want to contain the first number of the series.

2 Type the number (example: **1**). Then press **Enter**.

Note: Payroll and Cost of Goods data was added to the worksheet.

3 Click the cell (example: **G4**) you want to contain the second number of the series.

4 Type the number (example: **2**). Then press **Enter**.

Delete | Delete Data

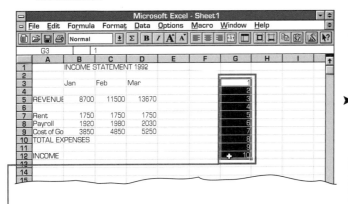

1 Select the cells you want to delete (example: **G3** to **G12**).

Note: To select cells, refer to page 10.

2 Press the **Delete** key and the **Clear** dialog box appears.

3 Click the **OK** button, or press **Enter**.

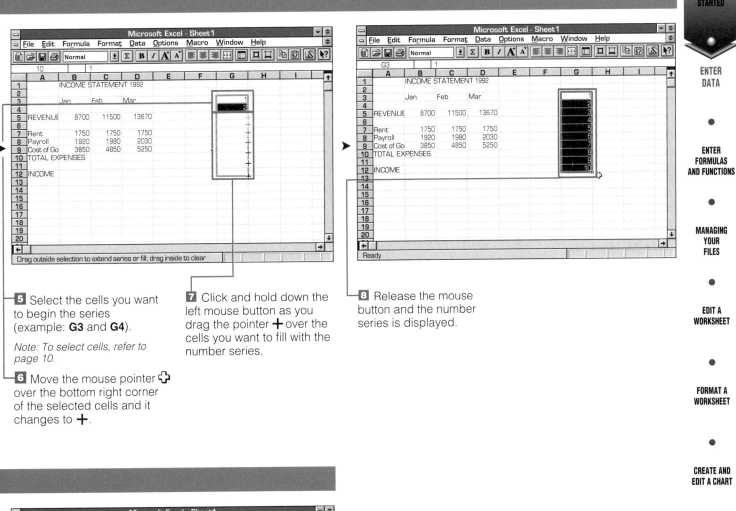

5 Select the cells you want to begin the series (example: **G3** and **G4**).

Note: To select cells, refer to page 10.

6 Move the mouse pointer ⬦ over the bottom right corner of the selected cells and it changes to ✛.

7 Click and hold down the left mouse button as you drag the pointer ✛ over the cells you want to fill with the number series.

8 Release the mouse button and the number series is displayed.

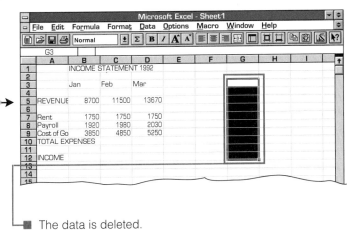

■ The data is deleted.

GETTING
STARTED

ENTER
DATA

ENTER
FORMULAS
AND FUNCTIONS

MANAGING
YOUR
FILES

EDIT A
WORKSHEET

FORMAT A
WORKSHEET

CREATE AND
EDIT A CHART

PRINT

OUTLINE A
WORKSHEET

CREATE AND
USE A
DATABASE

21

ORDER OF PRECEDENCE

■ Microsoft Excel performs operations in formulas based on the order of precedence.

■ Mathematical operators are included in formulas:

+	Add
*****	Multiply
–	Subtract
/	Divide

OPERATION	ORDER OF PRECEDENCE

Multiplication 1 ⎫
Division 1 ⎬ Done in order of appearance

Addition 2 ⎫
Subtraction 2 ⎬ Done in order of appearance

Example: *15-3*4 is executed as follows:*
-3*4+15=3

Example: *18/2*3 is executed as follows:*
18/2*3=27

Example: *1+2+3*4 is executed as follows:*
3*4+1+2=15

OVERRIDING THE ORDER OF PRECEDENCE

To override the order of precedence, parentheses can be used:

Examples:

Formula	Execution
E5-E7*E9	15-3*4=3
(E5-E7)*E9	(15-3)*4=48
G5/H2*H7	18/2*3=27
G5/(H2*H7)	18/(2*3)=3
J5+J6+J7*J9	1+2+3*4=15
(J5+J6+J7)*J9	(1+2+3)*4=24

■ A formula performs calculations and contains mathematical operators, numbers and cell references.

■ Cell references are normally used in formulas instead of numbers. Then, if the numbers in the cells change, the formula automatically recalculates the new result.

■ The formula appears at the top of the screen when the cell containing the formula is active (example: **B11**).

■ A formula always starts with an equal sign **=**.

■ The result of the calculation appears in the cell containing the formula (example: **B11**).

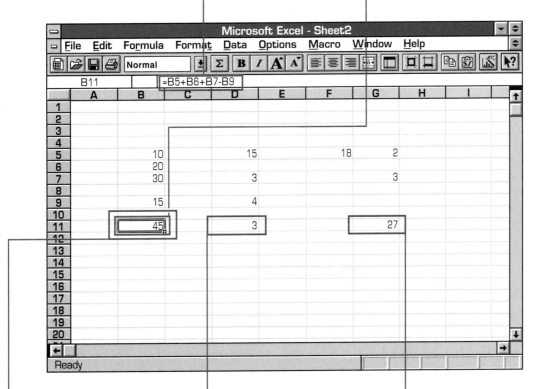

GETTING STARTED

ENTER DATA

ENTER FORMULAS AND FUNCTIONS

MANAGING YOUR FILES

EDIT A WORKSHEET

FORMAT A WORKSHEET

CREATE AND EDIT A CHART

PRINT

OUTLINE A WORKSHEET

CREATE AND USE A DATABASE

■ =B5+B6+B7-B9

The cell reference B11 contains this formula.

If: B5=10
       B6=20
       B7=30
       B9=15

Then: The formula calculates 45.

B11=10+20+30-15=45

■ =D5-D7*D9

The cell reference D11 contains this formula.

If: D5=15
       D7=3
       D9=4

Then: The formula calculates 3.

D11=15-3*4=3

■ =F5/G5*G7

The cell reference G11 contains this formula.

If: F5=18
       G5=2
       G7=3

Then: The formula calculates 27.

G11=18/2*3=27

ENTER FORMULAS AUTOFILL FORMULAS

Enter Formulas

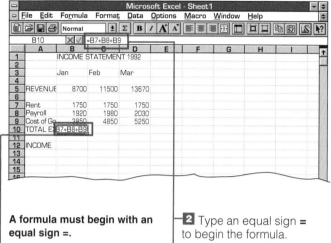

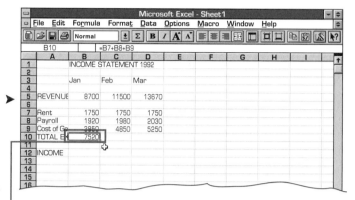

A formula must begin with an equal sign =.

1 Select the cell (example: **B10**) you want to enter a formula into.

2 Type an equal sign **=** to begin the formula.

3 Type the formula (example: to determine the Total Expenses, type **B7+B8+B9**).

4 Press **Enter**, and the result of the calculation is displayed (example: **7520**)

*Note: You can insert cell references into a formula by selecting the cells rather than typing them. For example, to add cells **B7**, **B8** and **B9**, click cell **B10** to select it. Then type an equal sign **=** to begin the formula. Click cell **B7**, then type a plus sign **+**. Click cell **B8**, then type a plus sign **+**. Click cell **B9**, then press **Enter**.*

AutoFill Formulas

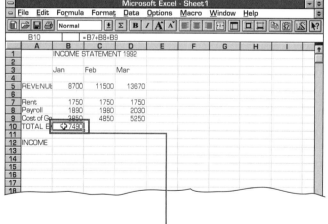

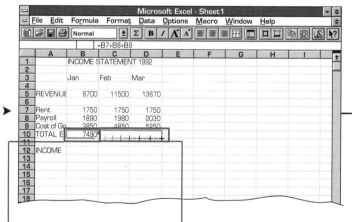

By using the AutoFill feature, Microsoft Excel can automatically copy a formula to all selected cells.

1 Click the cell (example: **B10**) that contains the formula you want to copy to other cells.

2 Move the mouse pointer ⇩ over the bottom right corner of the cell and it changes to **+**.

3 Click and hold down the left mouse button as you drag the pointer **+** over the cells you want to copy the formula to.

INTRODUCTION
TO FORMULAS

**ENTER
FORMULAS**

**AUTOFILL
FORMULAS**

INTRODUCTION
TO FUNCTIONS

ENTER
FUNCTIONS

SUM USING
THE AUTOSUM
TOOL

AUTOFILL
FUNCTIONS

ABSOLUTE
REFERENCES

GETTING
STARTED

ENTER
DATA

ENTER
FORMULAS
AND FUNCTIONS

MANAGING
YOUR
FILES

EDIT A
WORKSHEET

FORMAT A
WORKSHEET

CREATE AND
EDIT A CHART

PRINT

OUTLINE A
WORKSHEET

CREATE AND
USE A
DATABASE

Automatic Recalculation

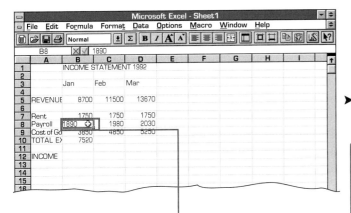

Cell references are normally used in formulas instead of numbers. Then, if the numbers in the cells change, the formula automatically recalculates the new result.

1 Select the cell (example: **B8**) you want to edit.

2 Type the new number (example: **1890**).

3 Press **Enter**, and the formula recalculates the new result (example: **7490**).

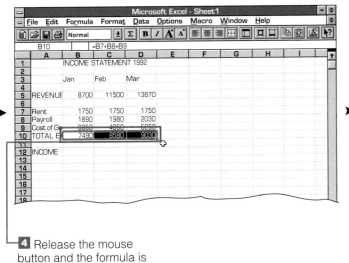

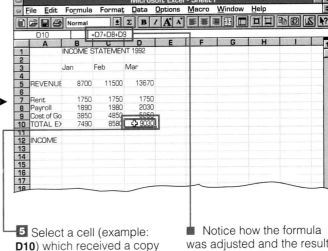

4 Release the mouse button and the formula is copied to all selected cells.

5 Select a cell (example: **D10**) which received a copy of the formula.

■ Notice how the formula was adjusted and the result recalculated for that cell.

INTRODUCTION TO FUNCTIONS

■ Functions are formulas built into Microsoft Excel to perform time-saving set-up procedures.

■ Functions begin with the equal sign **=**.

■ The function name (example: **SUM**) can be typed in either upper or lower case, but spaces between characters are not allowed.

■ A function argument (example: **B6:B9**), enclosed in parentheses **( )**, specifies the data the function works on. Arguments can consist of numbers or cell references.

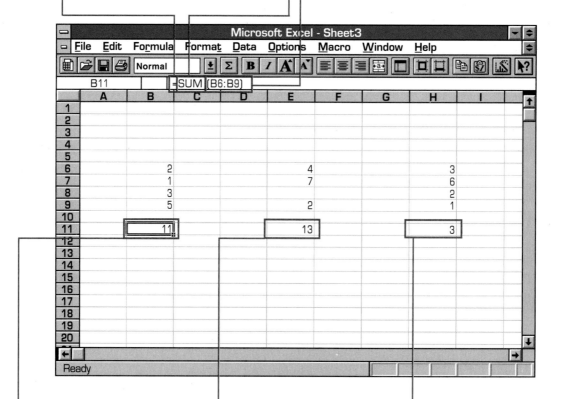

■ =SUM(B6:B9)

The cell reference B11 contains this function.

If:	B6 = 2
	B7 = 1
	B8 = 3
	B9 = 5
Then:	The function calculates 11.

B11=2+1+3+5=11

■ =SUM(E6,E7,E9)

The cell reference E11 contains this function.

If:	E6 = 4
	E7 = 7
	E9 = 2
Then:	The function calculates 13.

E11=4+7+2=13

■ =AVERAGE(H6:H9)

The cell reference H11 contains this function.

If:	H6 = 3
	H7 = 6
	H8 = 2
	H9 = 1
Then:	The function calculates 3.

H11=(3+6+2+1)/4=3

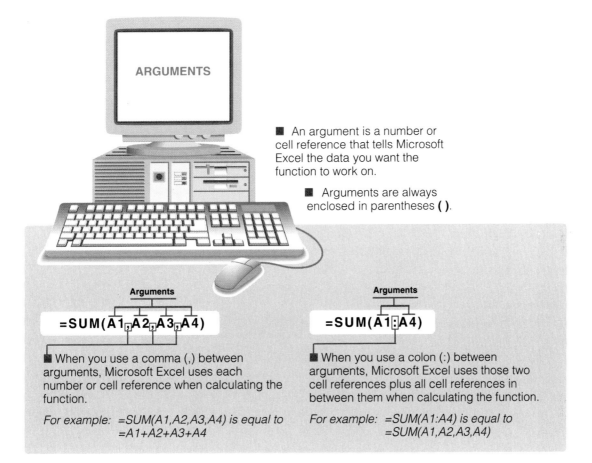

■ An argument is a number or cell reference that tells Microsoft Excel the data you want the function to work on.

■ Arguments are always enclosed in parentheses **( )**.

Arguments

=SUM(A1,A2,A3,A4)

■ When you use a comma (,) between arguments, Microsoft Excel uses each number or cell reference when calculating the function.

For example: =SUM(A1,A2,A3,A4) is equal to
=A1+A2+A3+A4

Arguments

=SUM(A1:A4)

■ When you use a colon (:) between arguments, Microsoft Excel uses those two cell references plus all cell references in between them when calculating the function.

For example: =SUM(A1:A4) is equal to
=SUM(A1,A2,A3,A4)

TYPICAL FUNCTIONS

SUM	Adds together the data in a list of values. *Example:* =SUM(C1:C9)	**MAX**	Finds the largest value in a list of values. *Example:* =MAX(B2:B70)
AVERAGE	Averages the data in a list of values. *Example:* =AVERAGE(B1:B6)	**MIN**	Finds the smallest value in a list of values. *Example:* =MIN(B2:B70)
DAYS360	Calculates the number of days between two dates. *Example:* =DAYS360("8/1/92","8/15/92") =14	**MEDIAN**	Finds the middle value in a list of values. *Example:* =MEDIAN(B2:B70)

Note: For a complete list of Functions, refer to the Microsoft Excel Function Reference guide.

GETTING STARTED

ENTER DATA

ENTER FORMULAS AND FUNCTIONS

MANAGING YOUR FILES

EDIT A WORKSHEET

FORMAT A WORKSHEET

CREATE AND EDIT A CHART

PRINT

OUTLINE A WORKSHEET

CREATE AND USE A DATABASE

Enter Functions

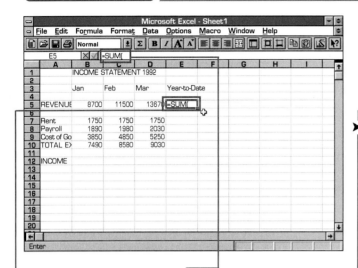

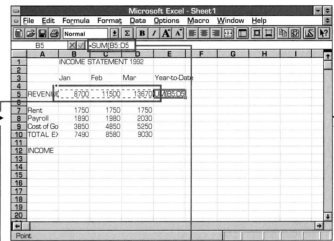

In the following example, the SUM function will be used to determine the total revenue.

*Note: The **Year-to-Date** column heading was entered into cell **E3**.*

1 Select the cell (example: **E5**) you want to enter the function into.

2 Type an equal sign **=** to begin the function.

3 Type the function name (example: **SUM**). Then type an open parenthesis **(**.

4 Click and hold down the left mouse button as you drag over the cells containing the numbers you want the function to work on (example: **B5** to **D5**). A dotted line appears around the selected cells.

5 Release the mouse button and the selected cells (example: **B5:D5**) are displayed in the formula bar.

*Note: You can also use the keyboard to specify which cells you want the function to work on (example: type **B5:D5**). For more information on arguments, refer to page 27.*

Σ Sum Using the AutoSum Tool

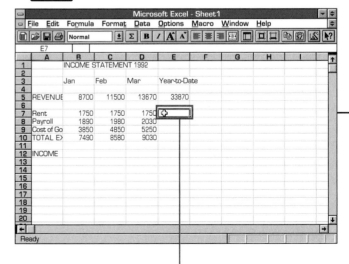

The AutoSum tool can quickly add a single row or column of data.

1 Click the cell (example: **E7**) you want to display the result of the added data.

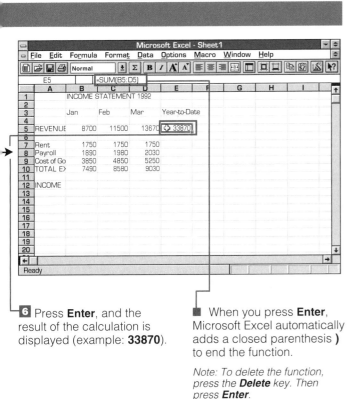

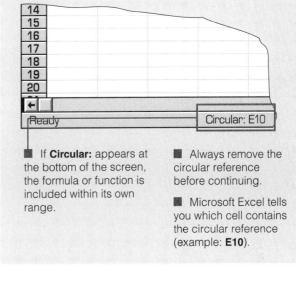

■ If **Circular:** appears at the bottom of the screen, the formula or function is included within its own range.

■ Always remove the circular reference before continuing.

■ Microsoft Excel tells you which cell contains the circular reference (example: **E10**).

6 Press **Enter**, and the result of the calculation is displayed (example: **33870**).

■ When you press **Enter**, Microsoft Excel automatically adds a closed parenthesis **)** to end the function.

*Note: To delete the function, press the **Delete** key. Then press **Enter**.*

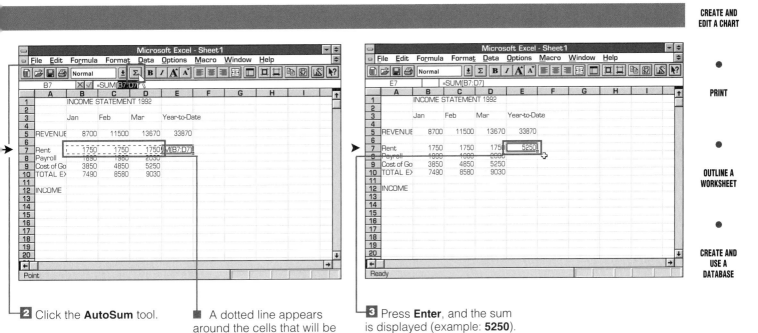

2 Click the **AutoSum** tool.

■ A dotted line appears around the cells that will be used to calculate the sum.

3 Press **Enter**, and the sum is displayed (example: **5250**).

GETTING STARTED

ENTER DATA

ENTER FORMULAS AND FUNCTIONS

MANAGING YOUR FILES

EDIT A WORKSHEET

FORMAT A WORKSHEET

CREATE AND EDIT A CHART

PRINT

OUTLINE A WORKSHEET

CREATE AND USE A DATABASE

AUTOFILL FUNCTIONS   ABSOLUTE REFERENCES

AutoFill Functions

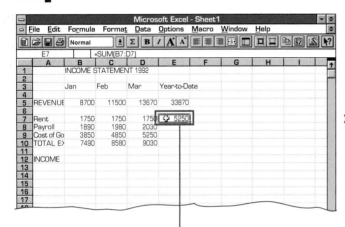

By using the AutoFill feature, Microsoft Excel can automatically copy a function to all selected cells.

1 Click the cell (example: **E7**) that contains the function you want to copy to other cells.

2 Move the mouse pointer ⊹ over the bottom right corner of the cell you want to copy and it changes to **+**.

3 Click and hold down the left mouse button as you drag the pointer **+** over the cells you want to copy the function to.

Absolute References

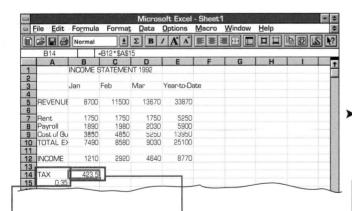
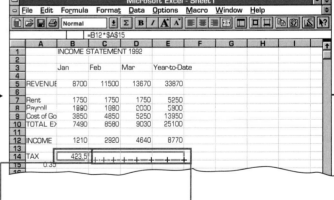

If a formula or function contains an absolute reference, Microsoft Excel will always use that same cell as a reference no matter where the formula or function is located in the worksheet.

1 Type and enter the data to be used as an absolute cell reference (example: **0.35** in cell **A15**).

2 Type and enter the formula containing the absolute reference (example: **=B12*A15** in cell **B14**).

Note: The $ signs tell Microsoft Excel that cell A15 is an absolute cell reference. This means the location of cell A15 (0.35) is fixed during the copying process.

3 To copy the formula to other cells, move the mouse pointer ⊹ over the bottom right corner of the cell you want to copy and it changes to **+**.

4 Click and hold down the left mouse button as you drag the pointer **+** over the cells you want to copy the formula (or function) to.

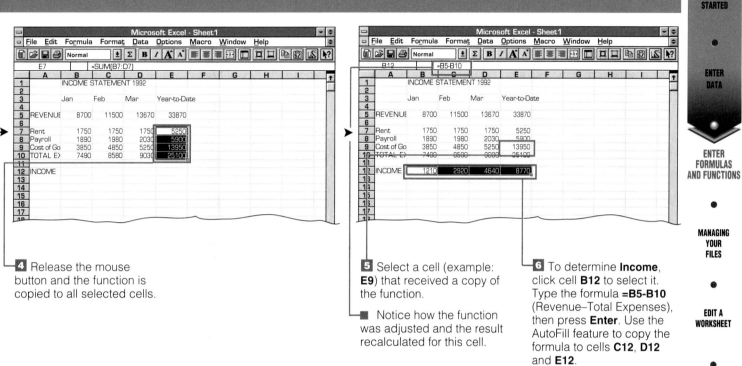

4 Release the mouse button and the function is copied to all selected cells.

5 Select a cell (example: **E9**) that received a copy of the function.

■ Notice how the function was adjusted and the result recalculated for this cell.

6 To determine **Income**, click cell **B12** to select it. Type the formula **=B5-B10** (Revenue–Total Expenses), then press **Enter**. Use the AutoFill feature to copy the formula to cells **C12**, **D12** and **E12**.

GETTING STARTED

ENTER DATA

ENTER FORMULAS AND FUNCTIONS

MANAGING YOUR FILES

EDIT A WORKSHEET

FORMAT A WORKSHEET

CREATE AND EDIT A CHART

PRINT

OUTLINE A WORKSHEET

CREATE AND USE A DATABASE

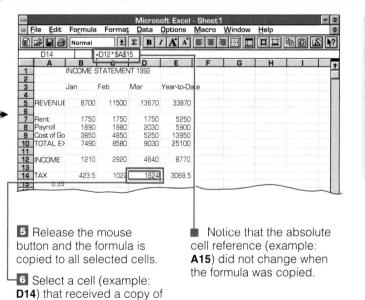

5 Release the mouse button and the formula is copied to all selected cells.

6 Select a cell (example: **D14**) that received a copy of the formula.

■ Notice that the absolute cell reference (example: **A15**) did not change when the formula was copied.

COPYING CELLS WITH ABSOLUTE REFERENCES

Example: **=B12*A15**

The first **$** sign tells Microsoft Excel that the column in the cell reference (example: **A**) is fixed. The second **$** sign tells Microsoft Excel that the row in the cell reference (example: **15**) is also fixed during the copy process.

FILES AND DIRECTORIES

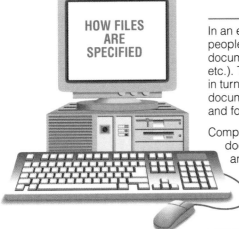

HOW FILES ARE SPECIFIED

In an efficient and productive office environment, people create, edit, review and organize paper documents (example: letters, worksheets, reports, etc.). These documents are stored in folders, which in turn are placed in cabinets. To retrieve a specific document, you must identify it by location (cabinet and folder) and then by name.

Computers work the same way. After creating a document in Microsoft Excel, it must be named and saved. During the save process, you must tell Microsoft Excel the drive (cabinet) and directory (folder) the file is to reside in.

Microsoft Excel uses a multilevel directory filing system to store and retrieve your programs and data files. The first level of this directory structure is called the root directory. From this directory other sudirectories may be created. A typical multilevel filing system is illustrated on the next page.

Note: The terms "directory" and "subdirectory" are used interchangeably. The "root directory" is the only directory that cannot be called a "subdirectory".

File Specification

A file is specified by describing its drive, path and name (filename and extension).

| C: | \EXCEL\EXAMPLES\ | INCOME92 | .XLS |

DRIVE

Tells Microsoft Excel the drive the file is in.

PATH

Tells Microsoft Excel the path through the directory structure to get to the file location.

FILENAME

The filename can contain up to 8 characters.

EXTENSION

The extension can contain up to 3 characters. In some cases, it is omitted.

Note: The first backslash (\) specifies the path to the root directory. Subsequent backslashes (\) are used to separate directories and the filename.

The following characters are allowed:

- The letters A to Z, upper or lower case
- The digits 0 through 9
- The underscore (_) and hyphen (-) characters
- The filename cannot contain a . (period) or blank spaces

FILES AND
DIRECTORIES

SAVE A
WORKSHEET

CLOSE A
WORKSHEET

OPEN A
SAVED
WORKSHEET

CREATE A
NEW
WORKSHEET

SWITCH
BETWEEN
WORKSHEETS

ARRANGE
WORKSHEETS

DELETE A
WORKSHEET

Using Directories to Organize Your Files

■ Directories can contain files and/or paths to other directories. In this example, the root directory has paths to three subdirectories.

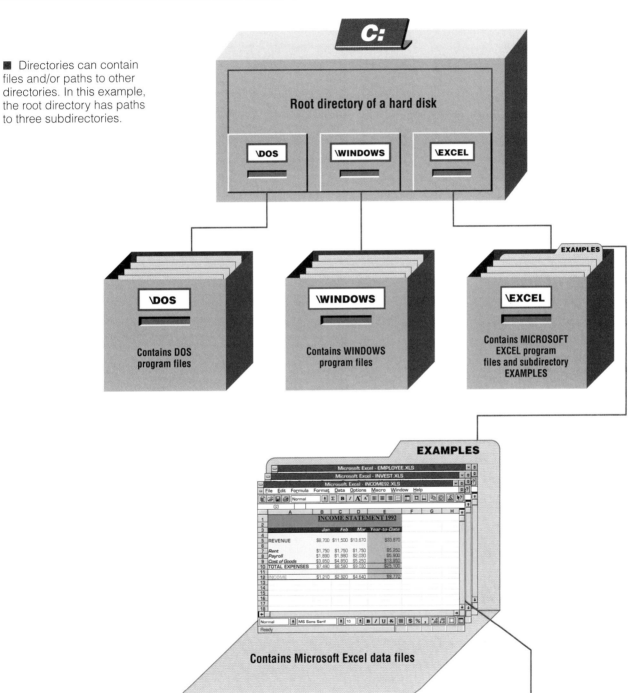

Root directory of a hard disk

\DOS

\WINDOWS

\EXCEL

EXAMPLES

\DOS

Contains DOS
program files

\WINDOWS

Contains WINDOWS
program files

\EXCEL

Contains MICROSOFT
EXCEL program
files and subdirectory
EXAMPLES

EXAMPLES

Contains Microsoft Excel data files

The file specification for this data file is:

C:\EXCEL\EXAMPLES\INCOME92.XLS

GETTING
STARTED

●

ENTER
DATA

●

ENTER
FORMULAS
AND FUNCTIONS

MANAGING
YOUR
FILES

●

EDIT A
WORKSHEET

●

FORMAT A
WORKSHEET

●

CREATE AND
EDIT A CHART

●

PRINT

●

OUTLINE A
WORKSHEET

●

CREATE AND
USE A
DATABASE

SAVE A WORKSHEET

Save a New Worksheet

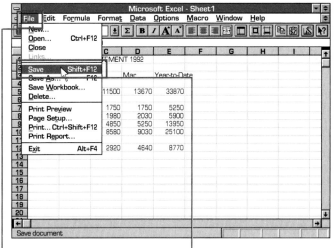

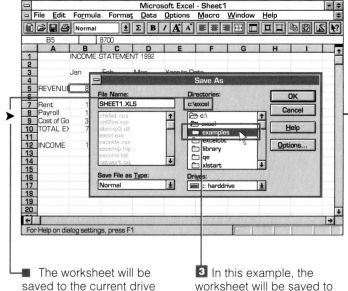

A worksheet must be saved before exiting Microsoft Excel if it is required for future use.

1 Click **File** to open its menu.

Note: The Tax data was deleted from the worksheet. To delete data, refer to page 20.

2 Click **Save** and the **Save As** dialog box appears.

*Note: To save a previously saved worksheet with a new name, click **File**, then click **Save As**. Then follow steps **3** to **5**.*

■ The worksheet will be saved to the current drive and directory (example: **c:\excel**).

3 In this example, the worksheet will be saved to the **examples** directory. To change to the **examples** directory, double click its name.

All examples in this guide are based on the directory structure illustrated below:

c: Root Directory	The **c:** drive contains the **excel** directory.
excel Microsoft Excel Directory	The **excel** directory stores the Microsoft Excel program files.
examples Microsoft Excel Data	In this guide the worksheet is saved to the **examples** directory which is located one level below the **excel** directory.

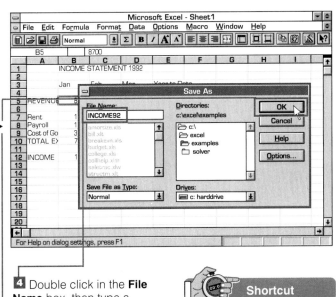

4 Double click in the **File Name** box, then type a name for your worksheet (example: **INCOME92**).

5 Click the **OK** button.

Shortcut

To replace steps **3** to **5**, you can type the file specification (example: **c:\excel\examples\income92**) in the **File Name** box. Then press **Enter**.

■ The file (example: **INCOME92.XLS**) is saved.

Note: If an extension is not specified, Microsoft Excel automatically adds the extension .XLS.

Save a Revised Worksheet

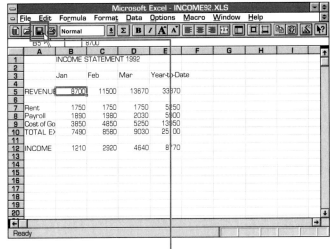

You should save regularly to prevent losing work due to power failure or hardware malfunctions.

1 Click the **Save File** tool to replace the previously saved version of the worksheet with the current one.

GETTING STARTED

●

ENTER DATA

●

ENTER FORMULAS AND FUNCTIONS

MANAGING YOUR FILES

●

EDIT A WORKSHEET

●

FORMAT A WORKSHEET

●

CREATE AND EDIT A CHART

●

PRINT

●

OUTLINE A WORKSHEET

●

CREATE AND USE A DATABASE

Save a Worksheet to a Different Drive

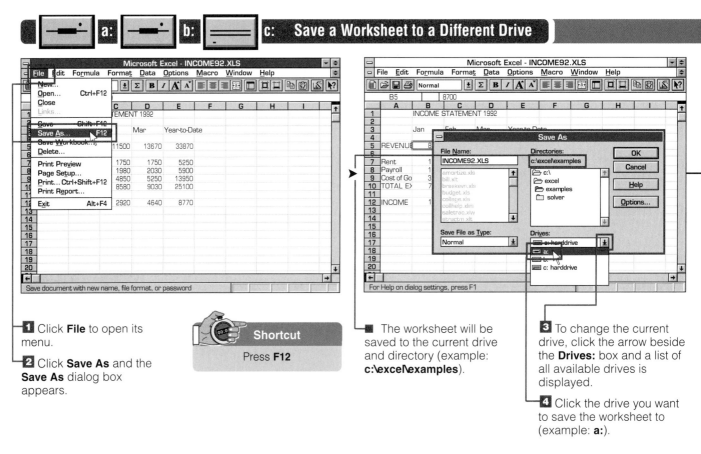

1 Click **File** to open its menu.

2 Click **Save As** and the **Save As** dialog box appears.

Shortcut

Press **F12**

■ The worksheet will be saved to the current drive and directory (example: **c:\excel\examples**).

3 To change the current drive, click the arrow beside the **Drives:** box and a list of all available drives is displayed.

4 Click the drive you want to save the worksheet to (example: **a:**).

Close a Worksheet

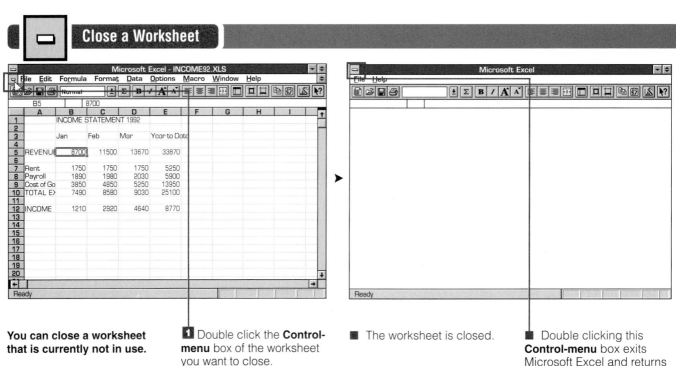

You can close a worksheet that is currently not in use.

1 Double click the **Control-menu** box of the worksheet you want to close.

■ The worksheet is closed.

■ Double clicking this **Control-menu** box exits Microsoft Excel and returns you to the Windows desktop.

FILES AND
DIRECTORIES

**SAVE A
WORKSHEET**

**CLOSE A
WORKSHEET**

OPEN A
SAVED
WORKSHEET

CREATE A
NEW
WORKSHEET

SWITCH
BETWEEN
WORKSHEETS

ARRANGE
WORKSHEETS

DELETE A
WORKSHEET

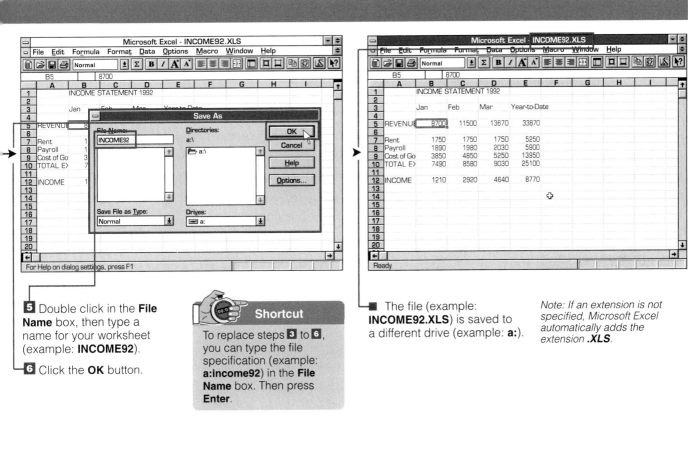

5 Double click in the **File Name** box, then type a name for your worksheet (example: **INCOME92**).

6 Click the **OK** button.

Shortcut

To replace steps **3** to **6**, you can type the file specification (example: **a:income92**) in the **File Name** box. Then press **Enter**.

■ The file (example: **INCOME92.XLS**) is saved to a different drive (example: **a:**).

*Note: If an extension is not specified, Microsoft Excel automatically adds the extension **.XLS**.*

If this dialog box appears when trying to close a worksheet, you have not saved changes you made to the worksheet.

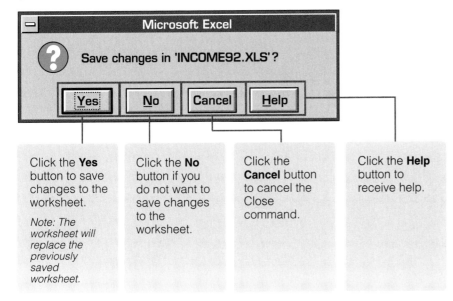

Click the **Yes** button to save changes to the worksheet.

Note: The worksheet will replace the previously saved worksheet.

Click the **No** button if you do not want to save changes to the worksheet.

Click the **Cancel** button to cancel the Close command.

Click the **Help** button to receive help.

GETTING
STARTED

●

ENTER
DATA

●

ENTER
FORMULAS
AND FUNCTIONS

MANAGING
YOUR
FILES

●

EDIT A
WORKSHEET

●

FORMAT A
WORKSHEET

●

CREATE AND
EDIT A CHART

●

PRINT

●

OUTLINE A
WORKSHEET

●

CREATE AND
USE A
DATABASE

Open a Saved Worksheet

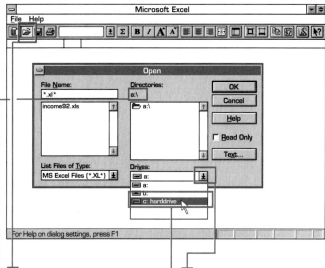

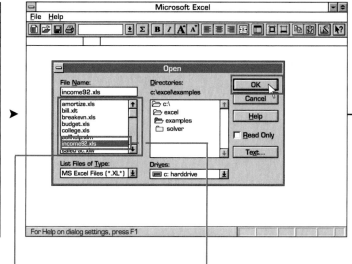

1 Click the **Open File** tool and the **Open** dialog box appears.

■ The current drive and directory are displayed (example: **a:**).

Note: The current drive and directory are the same as the last drive and directory that were opened or saved to.

2 To change the current drive, click the arrow beside the **Drives:** box and a list of all available drives is displayed.

3 Click the drive you want to change to (example: **c:**).

■ The files in the current drive and directory are displayed.

Note: To change the current directory, double click the directory you want to make current.

4 Click the name of the file you want to open (example: **income92.xls**).

5 Click the **OK** button, or press **Enter**.

Create a New Worksheet

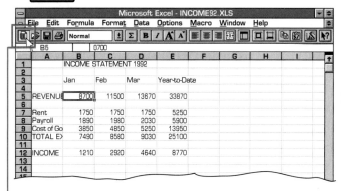

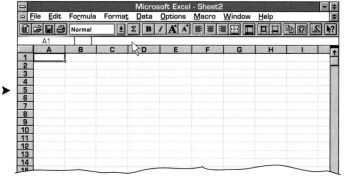

1 Click the **New Worksheet** tool.

■ A new worksheet appears.

*Note: The **INCOME92.XLS** worksheet is hidden behind the new worksheet.*

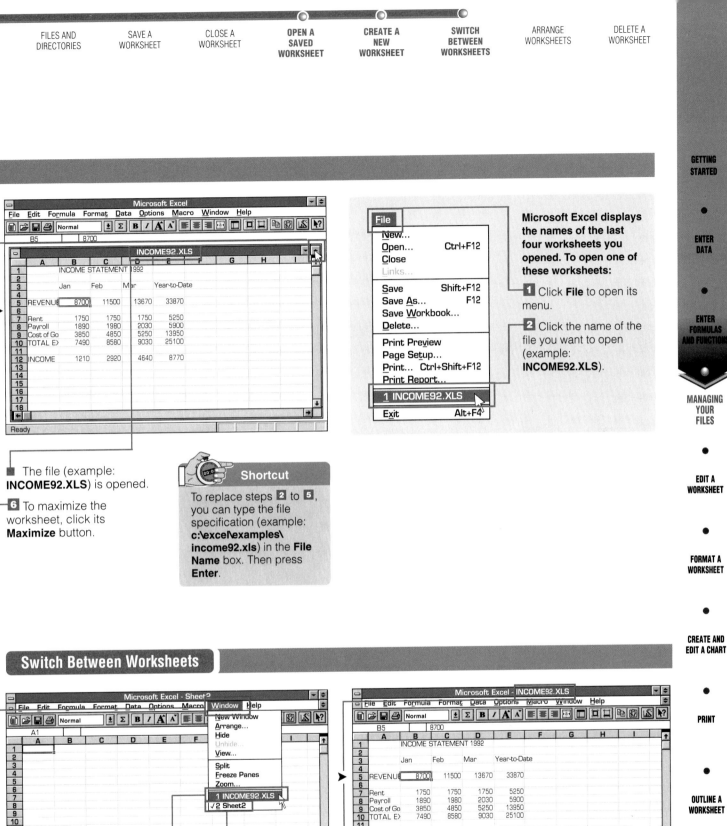

Microsoft Excel displays the names of the last four worksheets you opened. To open one of these worksheets:

1 Click **File** to open its menu.

2 Click the name of the file you want to open (example: **INCOME92.XLS**).

■ The file (example: **INCOME92.XLS**) is opened.

6 To maximize the worksheet, click its **Maximize** button.

Shortcut

To replace steps **2** to **5**, you can type the file specification (example: **c:\excel\examples\ income92.xls**) in the **File Name** box. Then press **Enter**.

GETTING STARTED

● ENTER DATA

● ENTER FORMULAS AND FUNCTIONS

MANAGING YOUR FILES

● EDIT A WORKSHEET

● FORMAT A WORKSHEET

● CREATE AND EDIT A CHART

● PRINT

● OUTLINE A WORKSHEET

● CREATE AND USE A DATABASE

Switch Between Worksheets

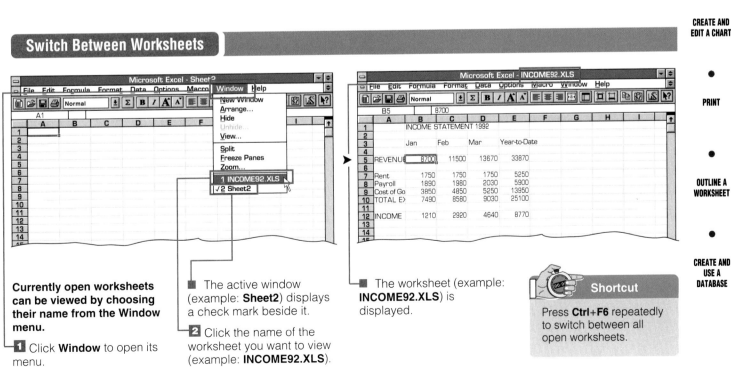

Currently open worksheets can be viewed by choosing their name from the Window menu.

1 Click **Window** to open its menu.

■ The active window (example: **Sheet2**) displays a check mark beside it.

2 Click the name of the worksheet you want to view (example: **INCOME92.XLS**).

■ The worksheet (example: **INCOME92.XLS**) is displayed.

Shortcut

Press **Ctrl+F6** repeatedly to switch between all open worksheets.

ARRANGE WORKSHEETS   DELETE A WORKSHEET

Arrange Worksheets

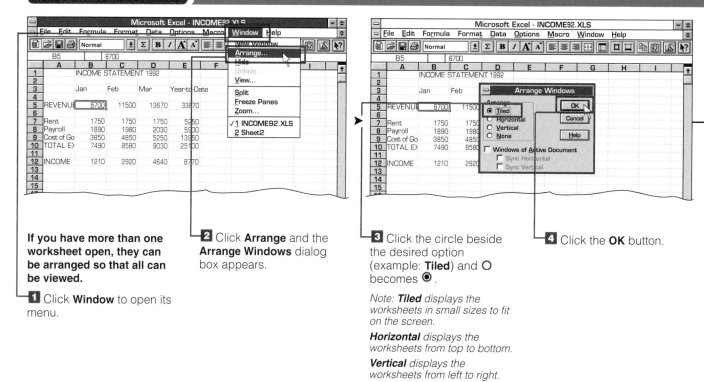

If you have more than one worksheet open, they can be arranged so that all can be viewed.

1 Click **Window** to open its menu.

2 Click **Arrange** and the **Arrange Windows** dialog box appears.

3 Click the circle beside the desired option (example: **Tiled**) and ○ becomes ◉ .

*Note: **Tiled** displays the worksheets in small sizes to fit on the screen.*

***Horizontal** displays the worksheets from top to bottom.*

***Vertical** displays the worksheets from left to right.*

4 Click the **OK** button.

Delete a Worksheet

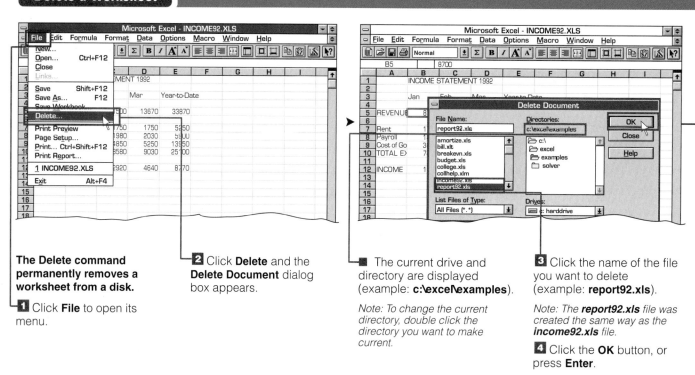

The Delete command permanently removes a worksheet from a disk.

1 Click **File** to open its menu.

2 Click **Delete** and the **Delete Document** dialog box appears.

■ The current drive and directory are displayed (example: **c:\excel\examples**).

Note: To change the current directory, double click the directory you want to make current.

3 Click the name of the file you want to delete (example: **report92.xls**).

*Note: The **report92.xls** file was created the same way as the **income92.xls** file.*

4 Click the **OK** button, or press **Enter**.

| FILES AND DIRECTORIES | SAVE A WORKSHEET | CLOSE A WORKSHEET | OPEN A SAVED WORKSHEET | CREATE A NEW WORKSHEET | SWITCH BETWEEN WORKSHEETS | **ARRANGE WORKSHEETS** | **DELETE A WORKSHEET** |

GETTING STARTED

ENTER DATA

ENTER FORMULAS AND FUNCTIONS

MANAGING YOUR FILES

EDIT A WORKSHEET

FORMAT A WORKSHEET

CREATE AND EDIT A CHART

PRINT

OUTLINE A WORKSHEET

CREATE AND USE A DATABASE

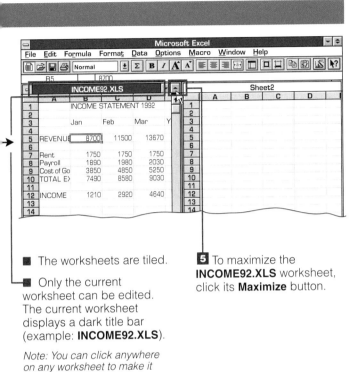

■ The worksheets are tiled.

■ Only the current worksheet can be edited. The current worksheet displays a dark title bar (example: **INCOME92.XLS**).

Note: You can click anywhere on any worksheet to make it current.

5 To maximize the **INCOME92.XLS** worksheet, click its **Maximize** button.

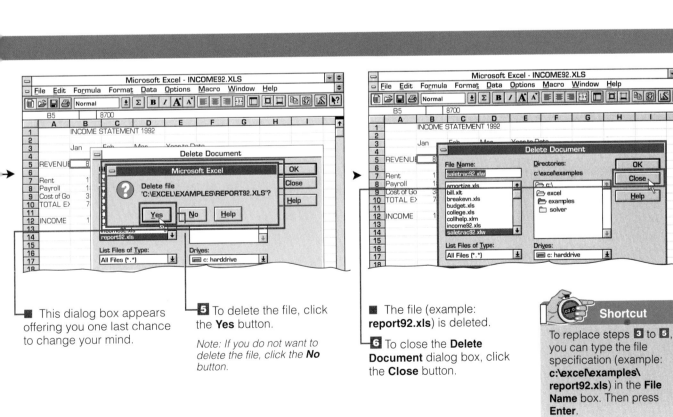

■ This dialog box appears offering you one last chance to change your mind.

5 To delete the file, click the **Yes** button.

*Note: If you do not want to delete the file, click the **No** button.*

■ The file (example: **report92.xls**) is deleted.

6 To close the **Delete Document** dialog box, click the **Close** button.

Shortcut

To replace steps **3** to **5**, you can type the file specification (example: **c:\excel\examples\ report92.xls**) in the **File Name** box. Then press **Enter**.

41

CHANGE COLUMN WIDTH

Change the Width of One Column

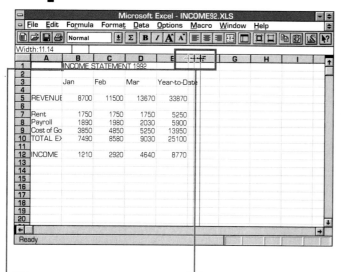

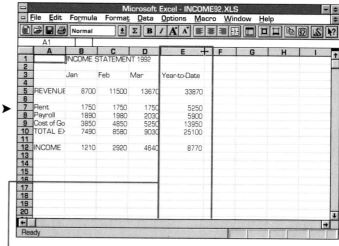

1 To change the width of a column (example: **E**), move the mouse pointer ⊹ over the right edge of the column heading and it changes to **+**.

2 Click and hold down the left mouse button as you drag the border to the desired width.

3 Release the mouse button and the column width is changed.

Note: When a number is too long to fit in a cell, Microsoft Excel tries to display it exponentially.

If the exponential form is still too long, number signs (###) are displayed in the cell.

To display the whole number, increase the column width.

Change the Width of Many Columns

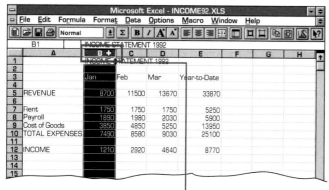

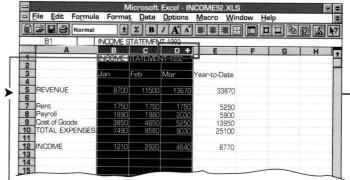

By changing the width of several columns at the same time, each selected column will end up displaying the same column width.

1 Click the column heading of the first column you want to change (example: **B**).

2 To select multiple adjacent columns, hold down the **Shift** key, then click the column heading of the last column you want to change (example: **D**). Release the **Shift** key.

*Note: To select nonadjacent columns, hold down the **Ctrl** key, then click the column headings you want to select.*

CHANGE
COLUMN
WIDTH

CHANGE
ROW HEIGHT

INSERT OR
DELETE A
ROW

INSERT OR
DELETE A
COLUMN

MOVE OR
COPY DATA

Best Fit the Width of One Column

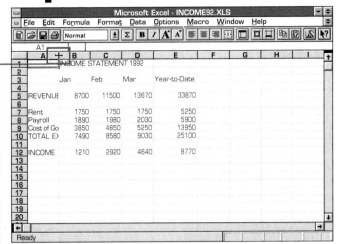
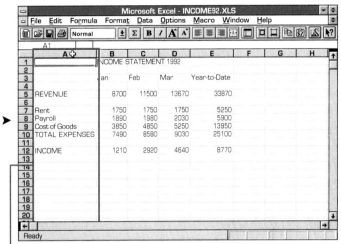

With Microsoft Excel you can easily change the column width to best fit the longest item in the column.

1 To best fit the width of a column (example: **A**), move the mouse pointer ✚ over the right edge of the column heading and it changes to ✚.

2 Double click the left mouse button.

■ The column width is changed to best fit the longest cell entry in the column (example: **TOTAL EXPENSES**).

3 To change the column width of all selected columns, move the mouse pointer ✚ over the right edge of any selected column heading (example: **D**) and it changes to ✚.

4 Click and hold down the left mouse button as you drag the border to the desired width.

5 Release the mouse button and all selected columns display the same column width.

GETTING
STARTED

ENTER
DATA

ENTER
FORMULAS
AND FUNCTIONS

MANAGING
YOUR
FILES

EDIT A
WORKSHEET

FORMAT A
WORKSHEET

CREATE AND
EDIT A CHART

PRINT

OUTLINE A
WORKSHEET

CREATE AND
USE A
DATABASE

43

CHANGE ROW HEIGHT

Change the Height of One Row

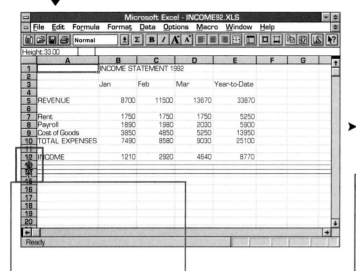

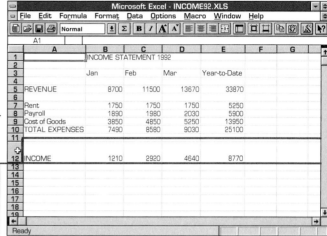

1 To change the height of a row (example: **12**), move the mouse pointer ✛ to the bottom edge of the row heading and it changes to ✢.

2 Click and hold down the left mouse button as you drag the border to the desired height.

3 Release the mouse button and the row height is changed.

Change the Height of Many Rows

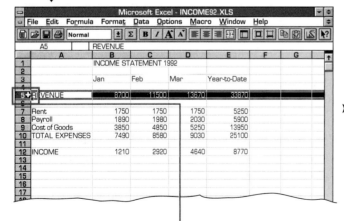

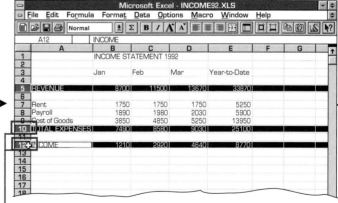

By changing the height of several rows at the same time, each selected row will end up displaying the same row height.

1 Click the row heading of the first row you want to change (example: **5**).

2 To select multiple nonadjacent rows, hold down the **Ctrl** key, then click the row headings you want to select (example: **10** and **12**). Release the **Ctrl** key.

*Note: To select adjacent rows, hold down the **Shift** key, then click the row heading of the last row you want to select. Release the **Shift** key.*

Best Fit the Height of One Row

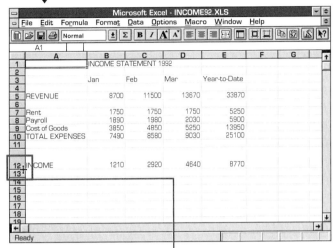

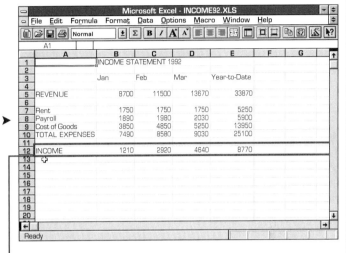

With Microsoft Excel you can easily change the row height to best fit the tallest item in the row.

1 To best fit the height of a row (example: **12**), move the mouse pointer ⊕ to the bottom edge of the row heading and it changes to ✛.

2 Double click the left mouse button.

■ The row height is changed to best fit the tallest cell entry in the row.

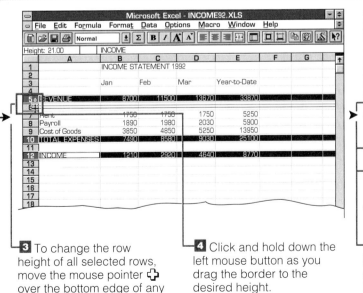

3 To change the row height of all selected rows, move the mouse pointer ⊕ over the bottom edge of any selected row heading (example: **5**) and it changes to ✛.

4 Click and hold down the left mouse button as you drag the border to the desired height.

5 Release the mouse button and all selected rows display the same row height.

GETTING STARTED

ENTER DATA

ENTER FORMULAS AND FUNCTIONS

MANAGING YOUR FILES

EDIT A WORKSHEET

FORMAT A WORKSHEET

CREATE AND EDIT A CHART

PRINT

OUTLINE A WORKSHEET

CREATE AND USE A DATABASE

Insert a Row

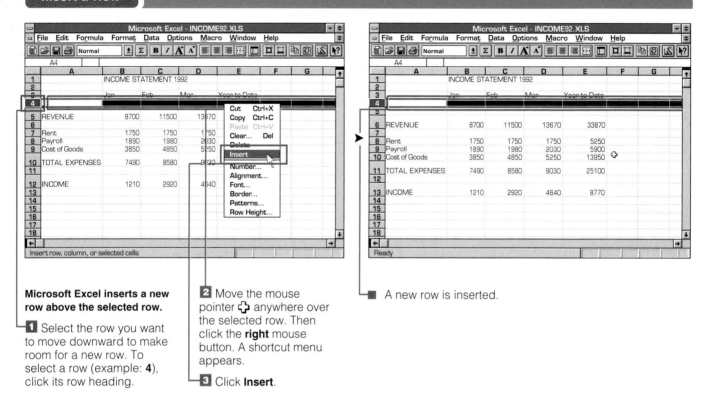

Microsoft Excel inserts a new row above the selected row.

1 Select the row you want to move downward to make room for a new row. To select a row (example: **4**), click its row heading.

2 Move the mouse pointer ⬦ anywhere over the selected row. Then click the **right** mouse button. A shortcut menu appears.

3 Click **Insert**.

■ A new row is inserted.

Delete a Row

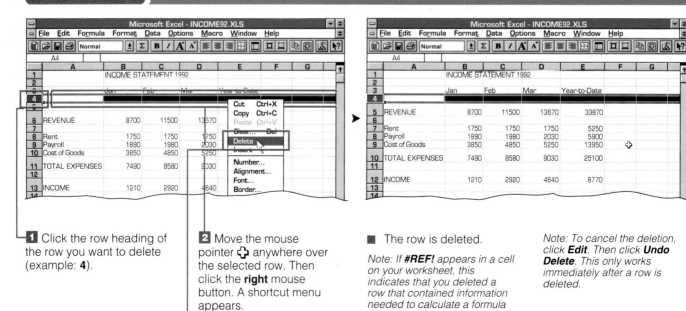

1 Click the row heading of the row you want to delete (example: **4**).

2 Move the mouse pointer ⬦ anywhere over the selected row. Then click the **right** mouse button. A shortcut menu appears.

3 Click **Delete**.

■ The row is deleted.

*Note: If **#REF!** appears in a cell on your worksheet, this indicates that you deleted a row that contained information needed to calculate a formula or function.*

*Note: To cancel the deletion, click **Edit**. Then click **Undo Delete**. This only works immediately after a row is deleted.*

CHANGE
COLUMN
WIDTH

CHANGE
ROW HEIGHT

INSERT OR
DELETE A
ROW

INSERT OR
DELETE A
COLUMN

MOVE OR
COPY DATA

Insert a Column

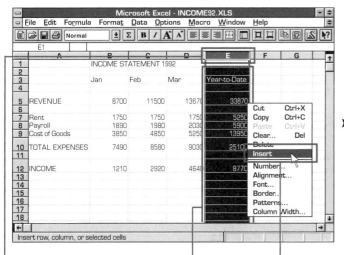

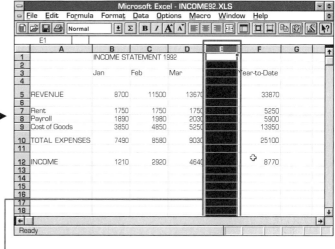

Microsoft Excel inserts a new column to the left of the selected column.

1 Select the column you want to move to the right to make room for a new column. To select a column (example: **E**), click its column heading.

2 Move the mouse pointer ✛ anywhere over the selected column. Then click the **right** mouse button. A shortcut menu appears.

3 Click **Insert**.

■ A new column is inserted.

Delete a Column

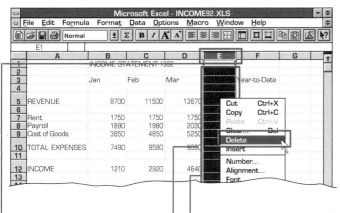

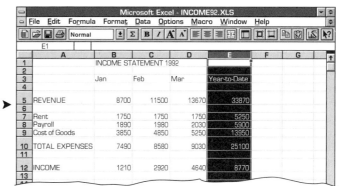

1 Click the column heading of the column you want to delete (example: **E**).

2 Move the mouse pointer ✛ anywhere over the selected column. Then click the **right** mouse button. A shortcut menu appears.

3 Click **Delete**.

■ The column is deleted.

*Note: If **#REF!** appears in a cell on your worksheet, this indicates that you deleted a column that contained information needed to calculate a formula or function.*

*Note: To cancel the deletion, click **Edit**. Then click **Undo Delete**. This only works immediately after a column is deleted.*

GETTING
STARTED

ENTER
DATA

ENTER
FORMULAS
AND FUNCTIONS

MANAGING
YOUR
FILES

EDIT A
WORKSHEET

FORMAT A
WORKSHEET

CREATE AND
EDIT A CHART

PRINT

OUTLINE A
WORKSHEET

CREATE AND
USE A
DATABASE

MOVE OR COPY DATA

Move Data

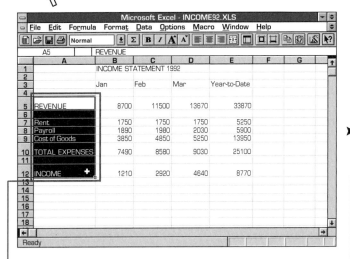

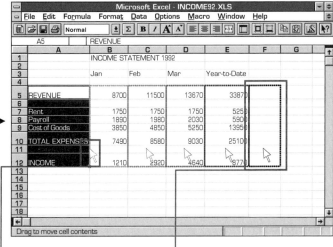

1 Select the cells you want to move to a new location.

Note: To select cells, refer to page 10.

2 Move the mouse pointer ⊕ over the border around the selected cells and it changes to ⇖.

3 Click and hold down the left mouse button as you drag the cells to the new location.

Copy Data

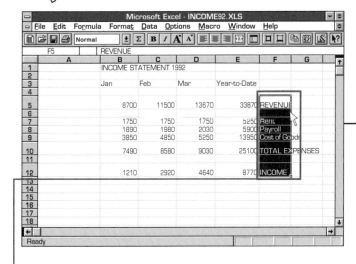

1 Select the cells you want to copy to a new location.

Note: To select cells, refer to page 10.

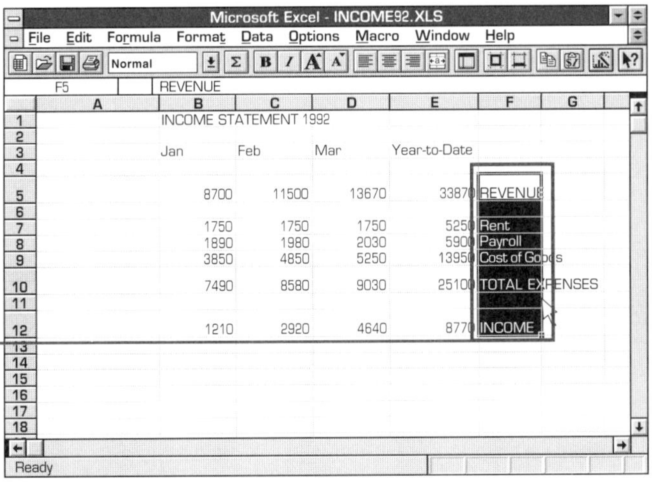
Microsoft Excel - INCOME92.XLS
File Edit Formula Format Data Options Macro Window Help
Normal
F5
REVENUE
INCOME STATEMENT 1992
Jan Feb Mar Year-to-Date
8700 11500 13670 33870 REVENUE
1750 1750 1750 5250 Rent
1890 1980 2030 5900 Payroll
3850 4850 5250 13950 Cost of Goods
7490 8580 9030 25100 TOTAL EXPENSES
1210 2920 4640 8770 INCOME
Ready

4 Release the mouse button and the data is moved.

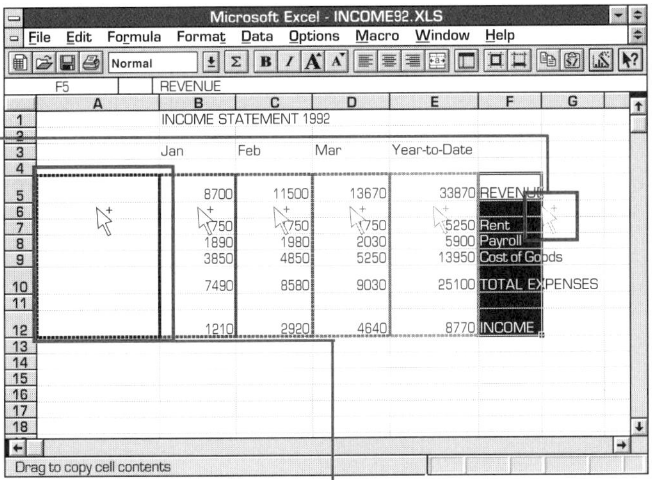
Microsoft Excel - INCOME92.XLS
File Edit Formula Format Data Options Macro Window Help
Normal
F5
REVENUE
INCOME STATEMENT 1992
Jan Feb Mar Year-to-Date
8700 11500 13670 33870 REVENUE
1750 1750 1750 5250 Rent
1890 1980 2030 5900 Payroll
3850 4850 5250 13950 Cost of Goods
7490 8580 9030 25100 TOTAL EXPENSES
1210 2920 4640 8770 INCOME
Drag to copy cell contents

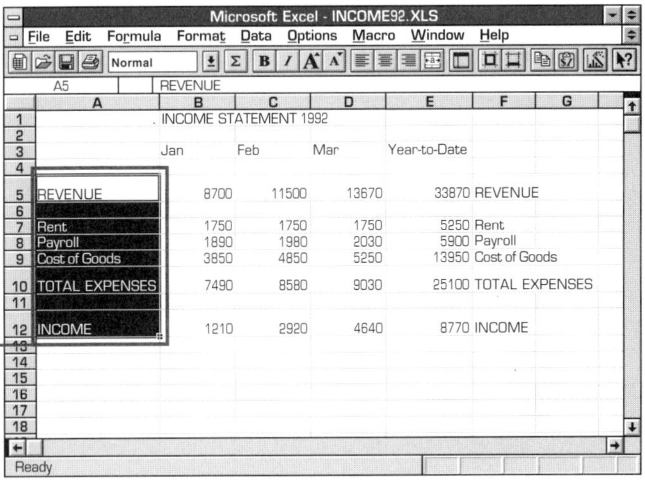
Microsoft Excel - INCOME92.XLS
File Edit Formula Format Data Options Macro Window Help
Normal
A5
REVENUE
INCOME STATEMENT 1992
Jan Feb Mar Year-to-Date
REVENUE 8700 11500 13670 33870 REVENUE
Rent 1750 1750 1750 5250 Rent
Payroll 1890 1980 2030 5900 Payroll
Cost of Goods 3850 4850 5250 13950 Cost of Goods
TOTAL EXPENSES 7490 8580 9030 25100 TOTAL EXPENSES
INCOME 1210 2920 4640 8770 INCOME
Ready

2 Move the mouse pointer ✥ over the border around the selected cells and it changes to ↖.

3 Press and hold down the **Ctrl** key and ↖ changes to ↖+.

4 Still holding down the **Ctrl** key, click and hold down the left mouse button as you drag the cells to the new location.

5 Release the mouse button, then the **Ctrl** key, and the data is copied.

MOVE OR COPY DATA

Move or Copy Data to Another Worksheet

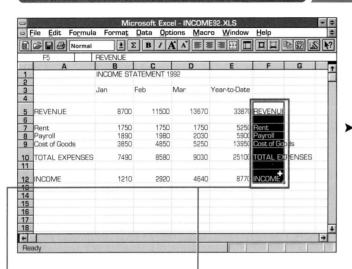

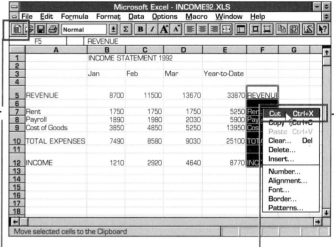

1 Select the cells you want to move (or copy) to a new location.

Note: To select cells, refer to page 10.

2 Move the mouse pointer ⊕ anywhere over the selected cells. Then click the **right** mouse button. A shortcut menu appears.

3 To move the selected cells, click **Cut**.

or

To copy the selected cells, click **Copy**.

4 To move (or copy) the data to a new worksheet, click the **New Worksheet** tool to open a new worksheet.

Note: You can also move (or copy) data to a saved worksheet by opening that worksheet. To open a saved worksheet, refer to page 38.

Rather than choosing a command from the main menu bar, you can use the **right** mouse button to display a shortcut menu.

A shortcut menu displays the most useful commands for that cell, cell range or object.

To display a shortcut menu, click the **right** mouse button over a selection or object.

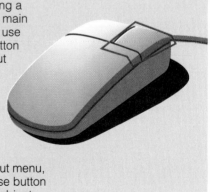

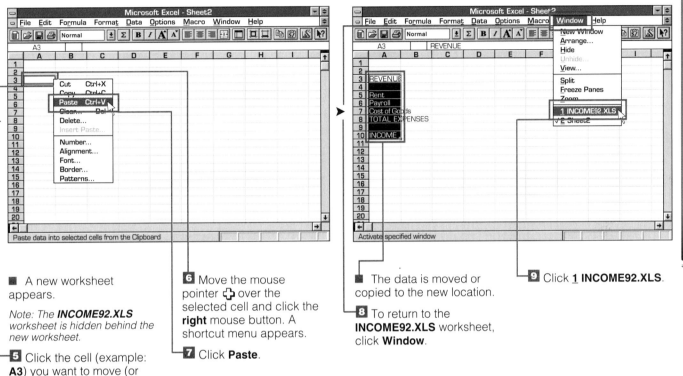

■ A new worksheet appears.

*Note: The **INCOME92.XLS** worksheet is hidden behind the new worksheet.*

5 Click the cell (example: **A3**) you want to move (or copy) the data to.

Note: The selected cell is used as the top left corner cell of the new location.

6 Move the mouse pointer ⊕ over the selected cell and click the **right** mouse button. A shortcut menu appears.

7 Click **Paste**.

■ The data is moved or copied to the new location.

8 To return to the **INCOME92.XLS** worksheet, click **Window**.

9 Click **1 INCOME92.XLS**.

GETTING STARTED

ENTER DATA

ENTER FORMULAS AND FUNCTIONS

MANAGING YOUR FILES

EDIT A WORKSHEET

FORMAT A WORKSHEET

CREATE AND EDIT A CHART

PRINT

OUTLINE A WORKSHEET

CREATE AND USE A DATABASE

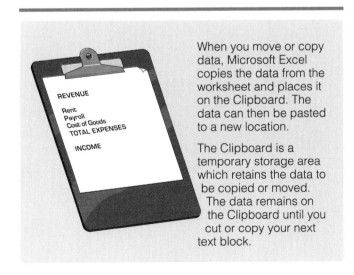

When you move or copy data, Microsoft Excel copies the data from the worksheet and places it on the Clipboard. The data can then be pasted to a new location.

The Clipboard is a temporary storage area which retains the data to be copied or moved. The data remains on the Clipboard until you cut or copy your next text block.

DISPLAY OR HIDE A TOOLBAR

FORMAT NUMBERS

Display or Hide a Toolbar

Toolbars contain tools that help you perform tasks quickly and more easily. Microsoft Excel offers the following toolbars:

TOOLBAR	DESCRIPTION
Standard	Contains tools for some of the most frequently used commands.
Formatting	Changes shape, size and general appearance of data.
Utility	Contains miscellaneous tools.
Chart	Changes chart appearance.
Drawing	Draws shapes, lines, and adds color.
Microsoft Excel 3.0	Contains the same tools as the Microsoft Excel Version 3.0 toolbar.

*Note: The **Macro** toolbar is for advanced users. For more information, refer to your Microsoft Excel User's Guides.*

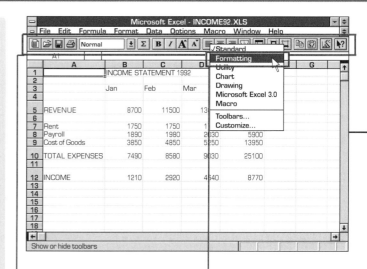

1 Move the mouse pointer ✛ anywhere over the **Standard** toolbar and it changes to ⃫ .

*Note: The **Standard** toolbar automatically appears when you first start Microsoft Excel.*

2 Click the **right** mouse button and a shortcut menu appears.

3 Click the name of the toolbar (example: **Formatting**) you want to display.

Note: A checkmark (✓) beside a toolbar name indicates it is already displayed. Click this toolbar name if you wish to hide it.

Format Numbers

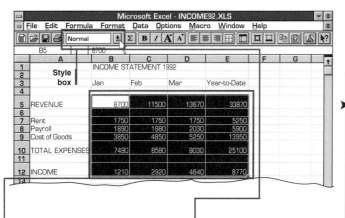

1 Select the cells that contain the numbers you want to format.

Note: To select cells, refer to page 10.

2 Click the arrow beside the **Style Box** and a list of the available styles appears.

*Note: You can use the **Style Box** on the **Standard** toolbar, or on the **Formatting** toolbar.*

3 Click the desired number style (example: **Currency [0]**).

Style Options	Shown As
Comma	1,000.00
Comma [0]	1,000
Currency	$1,000.00
Currency [0]	$1,000
Normal	1000
Percent	100000%

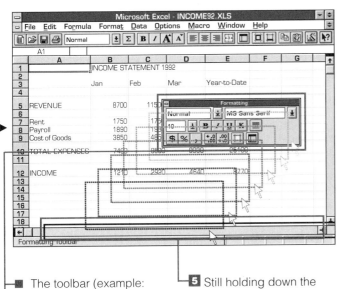

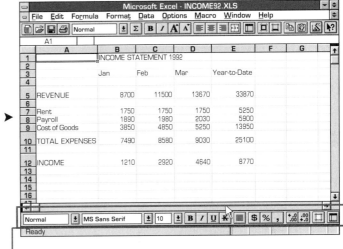

■ The toolbar (example: **Formatting**) is displayed.

4 To reposition the toolbar, move the mouse pointer over a blank area in the toolbar. Click the left mouse button and hold it down.

5 Still holding down the button, drag the toolbar to where you want it positioned.

6 Release the mouse button and the toolbar jumps to its new position.

Note: If you drag a toolbar to the top or bottom edge of the screen, it lines up along that edge.

Note: If you accidentally hide all the toolbars, click **Options***, then click* **Toolbars***. Double click the name of the toolbar you want to display.*

GETTING STARTED

●

ENTER DATA

●

ENTER FORMULAS AND FUNCTIONS

●

MANAGING YOUR FILES

●

EDIT A WORKSHEET

FORMAT A WORKSHEET

●

CREATE AND EDIT A CHART

●

PRINT

●

OUTLINE A WORKSHEET

●

CREATE AND USE A DATABASE

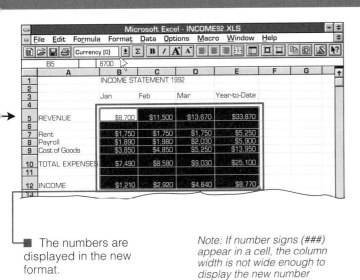

■ The numbers are displayed in the new format.

Note: If number signs (###) appear in a cell, the column width is not wide enough to display the new number format. To change the column width, refer to page 42.

FORMAT NUMBERS USING THE FORMATTING TOOLS

1 Select the cells that contain the numbers you want to format.

2 Click the desired format tool:

$	**Currency (2 decimal places)**
%	**Percent (0 decimal places)**
,	**Comma (2 decimal places)**
←.0 .00	**Add 1 decimal place to a number**
.00 →.0	**Remove 1 decimal place from a number**

Change Fonts

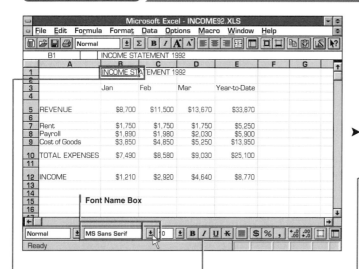

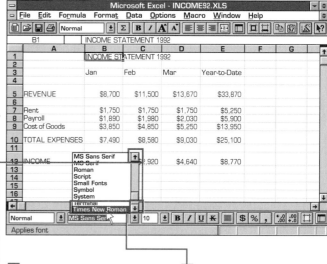

A font defines the design of displayed characters.

1 Select the cell(s) that contains the data you want to change to a new font (example: **B1**).

Note: To select cells, refer to page 10.

2 Click the arrow beside the **Font Name Box** and a list of the available fonts appears.

*Note: The **Font Name Box** is on the **Formatting** toolbar.*

3 To view more fonts, click the up ⬆ or down ⬇ scroll arrow.

4 Click the desired font name (example: **Times New Roman**).

Increase or Decrease Font Size

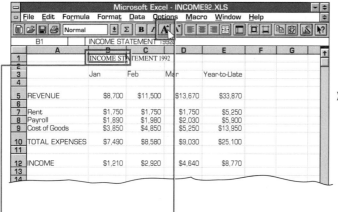

1 Select the cell(s) that contains the data you want to change to a new font size.

2 To increase the font size, click the **Increase Font Size** tool 🅰.

*Note: To decrease the font size, click the **Decrease Font Size** tool 🅰.*

■ The size of the text is changed.

Note: The size of numbers can also be changed.

3 Continue clicking a **Font Size** tool until the desired size is reached (example: click the **Increase Font Size** tool twice to move up two font sizes).

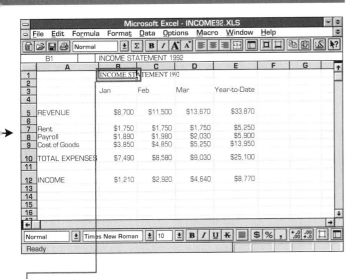

■ The text in the selected cell is displayed with the new font.

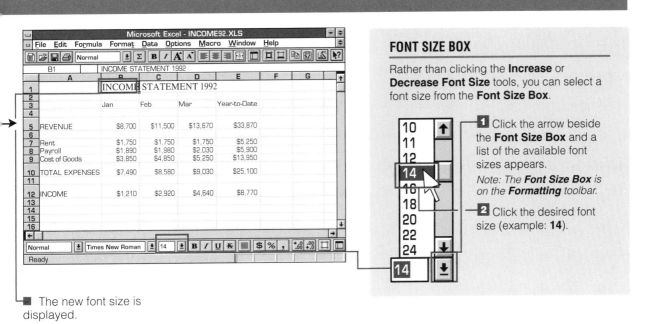

FONT SIZE BOX

Rather than clicking the **Increase** or **Decrease Font Size** tools, you can select a font size from the **Font Size Box**.

1 Click the arrow beside the **Font Size Box** and a list of the available font sizes appears.

Note: The Font Size Box is on the Formatting toolbar.

2 Click the desired font size (example: **14**).

■ The new font size is displayed.

GETTING STARTED

ENTER DATA

ENTER FORMULAS AND FUNCTIONS

MANAGING YOUR FILES

EDIT A WORKSHEET

FORMAT A WORKSHEET

CREATE AND EDIT A CHART

PRINT

OUTLINE A WORKSHEET

CREATE AND USE A DATABASE

Left **Center** **Right Align**

With Microsoft Excel you can left align, right align, or center data in each cell.

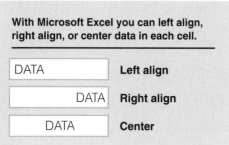

DATA	**Left align**
DATA	**Right align**
DATA	**Center**

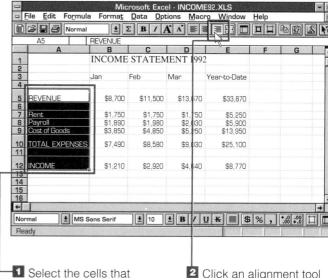

1 Select the cells that contain the data you want to align.

Note: To select cells, refer to page 10.

2 Click an alignment tool (example: **Right Align**).

*Note: The alignment tools are on the **Standard** toolbar.*

 Center Text Across Selected Columns

Before	Center text	
After		Center text

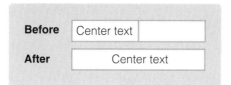

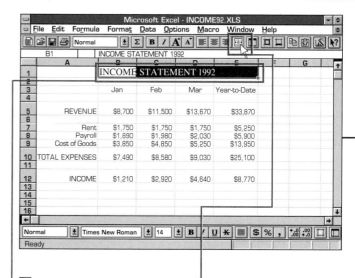

1 Select the cells you want the text to be centered between.

Note: Make sure the text you want to center across columns is in the far left selected cell.

2 Click the **Center Across Columns** tool.

*Note: This tool is on the **Standard** toolbar.*

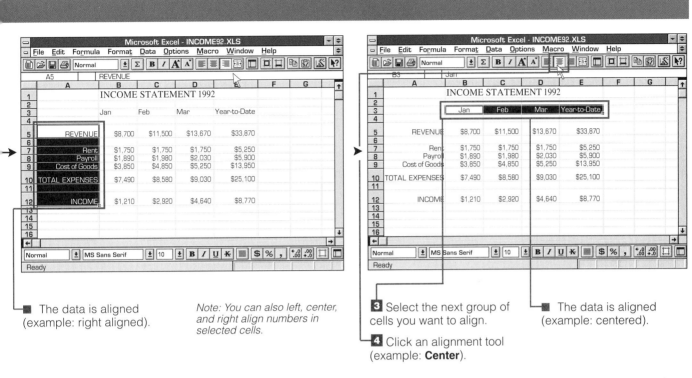

■ The data is aligned (example: right aligned).

Note: You can also left, center, and right align numbers in selected cells.

3 Select the next group of cells you want to align.

4 Click an alignment tool (example: **Center**).

■ The data is aligned (example: centered).

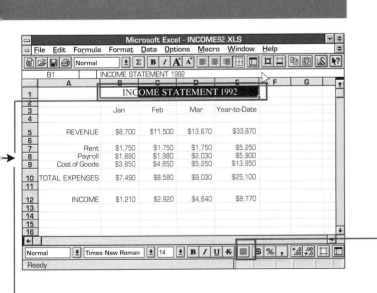

■ The text is centered between the selected columns.

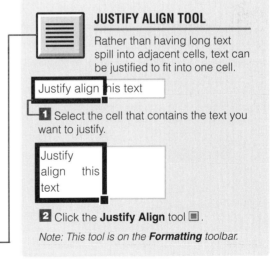

JUSTIFY ALIGN TOOL

Rather than having long text spill into adjacent cells, text can be justified to fit into one cell.

Justify align this text

1 Select the cell that contains the text you want to justify.

Justify align this text

2 Click the **Justify Align** tool ▤.

*Note: This tool is on the **Formatting** toolbar.*

GETTING STARTED

ENTER DATA

ENTER FORMULAS AND FUNCTIONS

MANAGING YOUR FILES

EDIT A WORKSHEET

FORMAT A WORKSHEET

CREATE AND EDIT A CHART

PRINT

OUTLINE A WORKSHEET

CREATE AND USE A DATABASE

BORDERS AND SHADING

REMOVE FORMATS

Add Borders

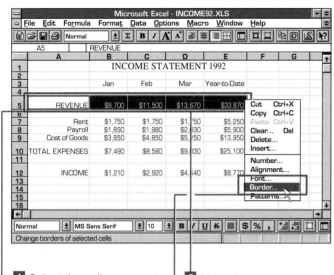

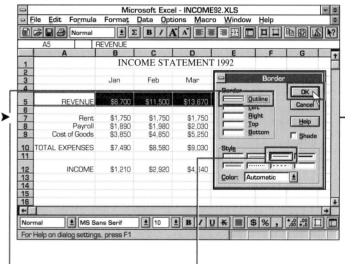

1 Select the cells you want to add a border to.

Note: To select cells, refer to page 10.

2 Move the mouse pointer ⊕ anywhere over the selected cells. Then click the **right** mouse button. A shortcut menu appears.

3 Click **Border** and the **Border** dialog box appears.

4 Click the desired border type (example: **Outline**).

Note: To deselect a line, click the border type again.

5 Click the desired line style.

*Note: To make a colored line, click the arrow beside **Color**: ⊡. Then click the desired color.*

6 Click the **OK** button, or press **Enter**.

Add Shading

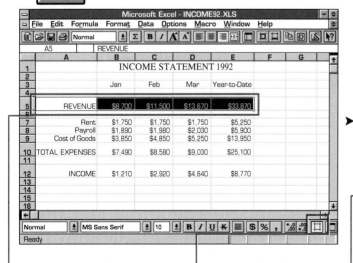

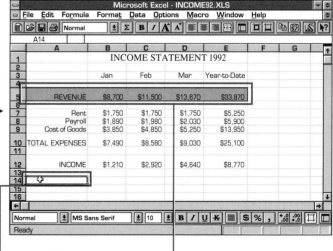

1 Select the cells you want to display with shading.

Note: To select cells, refer to page 10.

2 Click the **Light Shading** tool.

*Note: This tool is found on the **Formatting** toolbar.*

3 Click a cell outside the selected cell range (example: **A14**) so you can clearly view the shading.

■ The cells display the light shading pattern.

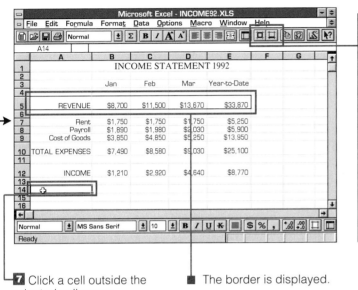

OUTLINE BORDER TOOL

To quickly add a border along the outermost edges of selected cells:

1 Select the cells you want to add the border to.

2 Click the **Outline Border** tool ▣.

*Note: This tool is found on the **Standard** toolbar.*

BOTTOM BORDER TOOL

To quickly add a border along the bottom edge of selected cells:

1 Select the cells you want to add the border to.

2 Click the **Bottom Border** tool ▣.

*Note: This tool is found on the **Standard** toolbar.*

7 Click a cell outside the selected cell range (example: **A14**) so you can clearly view the border.

■ The border is displayed.

GETTING STARTED

ENTER DATA

ENTER FORMULAS AND FUNCTIONS

MANAGING YOUR FILES

EDIT A WORKSHEET

FORMAT A WORKSHEET

CREATE AND EDIT A CHART

PRINT

OUTLINE A WORKSHEET

CREATE AND USE A DATABASE

Delete

Remove Formats

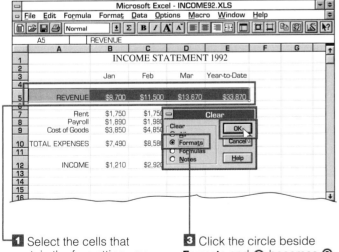

1 Select the cells that contain the formatting you want to remove.

Note: To select cells, refer to page 10.

2 Press the **Delete** key and the **Clear** dialog box appears.

3 Click the circle beside **Formats** and ○ becomes ◉.

4 Click the **OK** button, or press **Enter**.

5 Click a cell outside the selected cell range (example: **A14**) so you can clearly see that all formatting was removed.

■ All formats are cleared from the selected cells. The data within the cells does not change.

6 To quickly undo the remove formats command, press **Ctrl+Z**.

*Note: You can also undo the remove formats command by using the Main menu. Click **Edit**, then click **Undo Clear**.*

COPY AND PASTE FORMATS

BOLD, ITALIC, AND UNDERLINE

Copy and Paste Formats

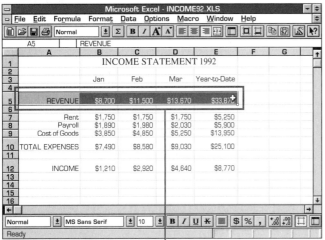

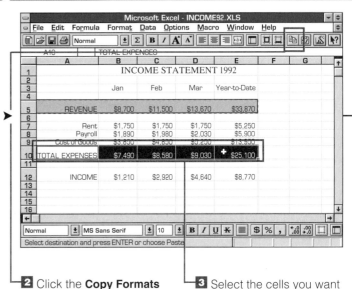

You can apply current formats quickly and consistently to selected cells by using the Copy and Paste Formats tools.

1 Select the cells that contain the format attributes you want to copy to other cells.

2 Click the **Copy Formats** tool.

Note: A moving border appears around the cells to be copied.

3 Select the cells you want to apply the format to.

Bold

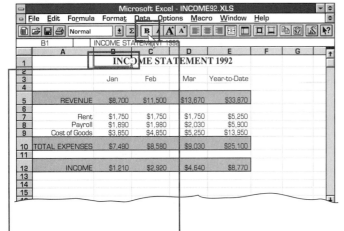

1 Select the cell(s) that contains the data you want to make bold.

2 Click the **Bold** tool.

*Note: The **Bold** tool is offered on both the **Standard** and **Formatting** toolbars. You can click either tool.*

*To remove the bold formatting from selected cells, click the **Bold** tool again.*

Italic

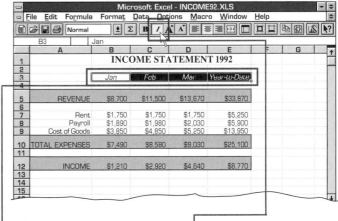

1 Select the cells that contain the data you want to make italic.

2 Click the **Italic** tool.

*Note: The **Italic** tool is offered on both the **Standard** and **Formatting** toolbars. You can click either tool.*

*To remove the italic formatting from selected cells, click the **Italic** tool again.*

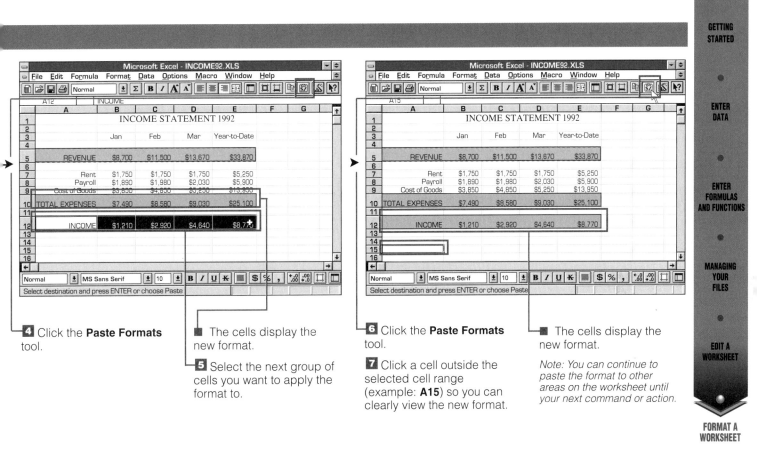

4 Click the **Paste Formats** tool.

■ The cells display the new format.

5 Select the next group of cells you want to apply the format to.

6 Click the **Paste Formats** tool.

7 Click a cell outside the selected cell range (example: **A15**) so you can clearly view the new format.

■ The cells display the new format.

Note: You can continue to paste the format to other areas on the worksheet until your next command or action.

GETTING STARTED

ENTER DATA

ENTER FORMULAS AND FUNCTIONS

MANAGING YOUR FILES

EDIT A WORKSHEET

FORMAT A WORKSHEET

CREATE AND EDIT A CHART

PRINT

OUTLINE A WORKSHEET

CREATE AND USE A DATABASE

Underline

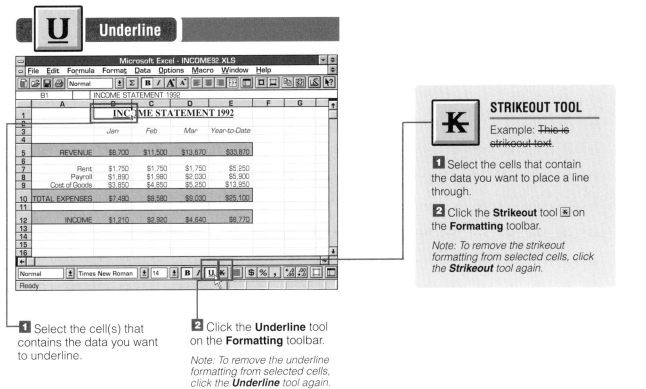

1 Select the cell(s) that contains the data you want to underline.

2 Click the **Underline** tool on the **Formatting** toolbar.

*Note: To remove the underline formatting from selected cells, click the **Underline** tool again.*

STRIKEOUT TOOL

Example: ~~This is strikeout text~~.

1 Select the cells that contain the data you want to place a line through.

2 Click the **Strikeout** tool on the **Formatting** toolbar.

*Note: To remove the strikeout formatting from selected cells, click the **Strikeout** tool again.*

AUTOFORMAT

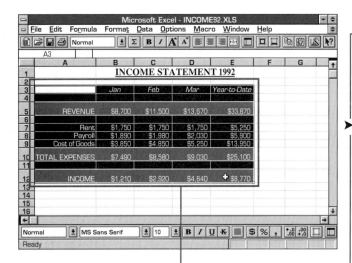

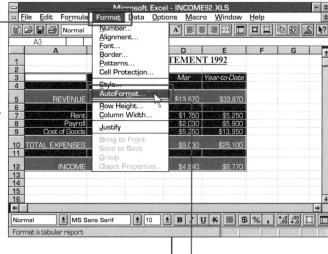

Microsoft Excel offers 14 different built-in formatting choices so you can quickly format your worksheet.

1 Select the cells you want to apply the AutoFormat to.

Note: To select cells, refer to page 10.

2 Click **Format** to open its menu.

3 Click **AutoFormat** and the **AutoFormat** dialog box appears.

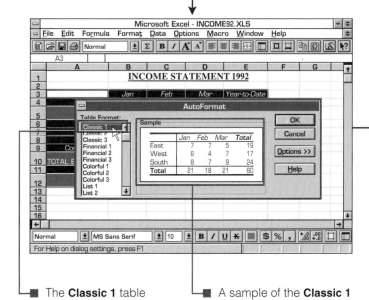

■ The **Classic 1** table format is the current selection.

■ A sample of the **Classic 1** AutoFormat appears in the **Sample** box.

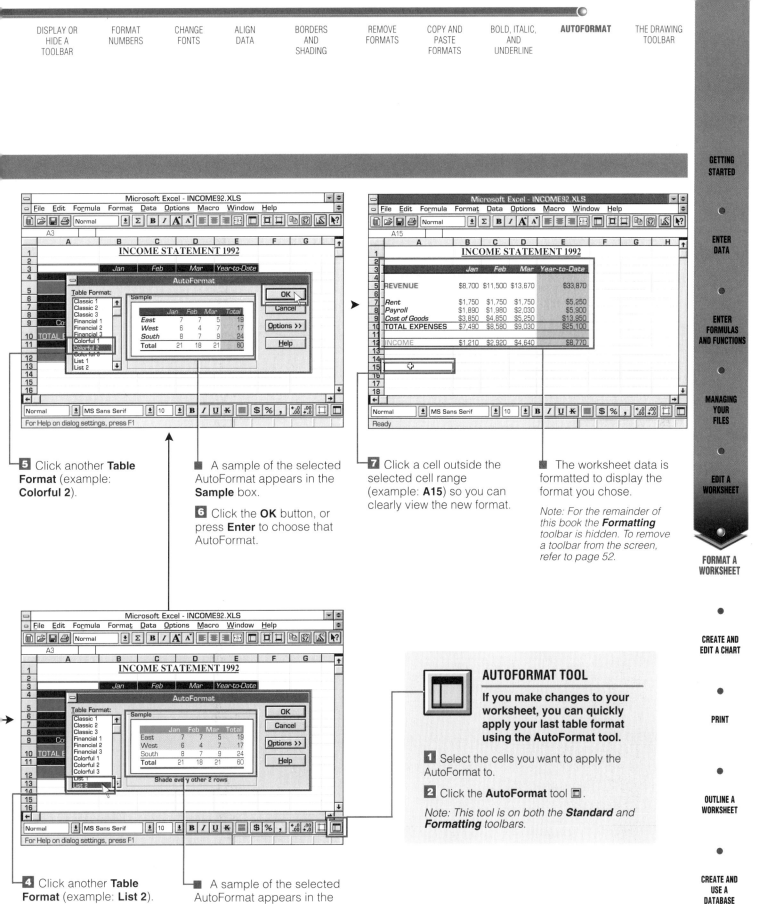

5 Click another **Table Format** (example: **Colorful 2**).

■ A sample of the selected AutoFormat appears in the **Sample** box.

6 Click the **OK** button, or press **Enter** to choose that AutoFormat.

7 Click a cell outside the selected cell range (example: **A15**) so you can clearly view the new format.

■ The worksheet data is formatted to display the format you chose.

*Note: For the remainder of this book the **Formatting** toolbar is hidden. To remove a toolbar from the screen, refer to page 52.*

4 Click another **Table Format** (example: **List 2**).

■ A sample of the selected AutoFormat appears in the **Sample** box.

AUTOFORMAT TOOL

If you make changes to your worksheet, you can quickly apply your last table format using the AutoFormat tool.

1 Select the cells you want to apply the AutoFormat to.

2 Click the **AutoFormat** tool □.

*Note: This tool is on both the **Standard** and **Formatting** toolbars.*

GETTING STARTED

ENTER DATA

ENTER FORMULAS AND FUNCTIONS

MANAGING YOUR FILES

EDIT A WORKSHEET

FORMAT A WORKSHEET

CREATE AND EDIT A CHART

PRINT

OUTLINE A WORKSHEET

CREATE AND USE A DATABASE

THE DRAWING TOOLBAR

Draw Shapes

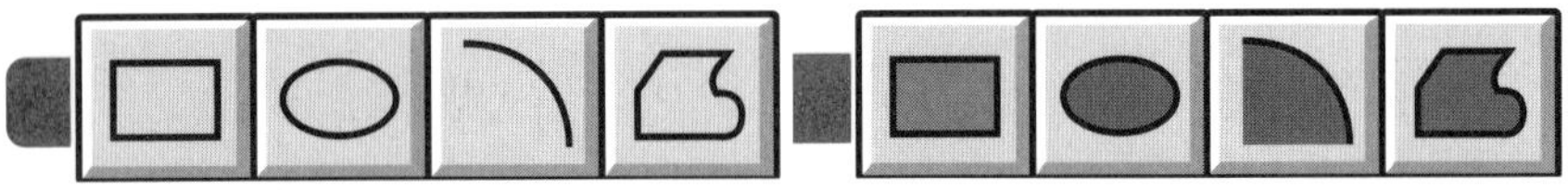

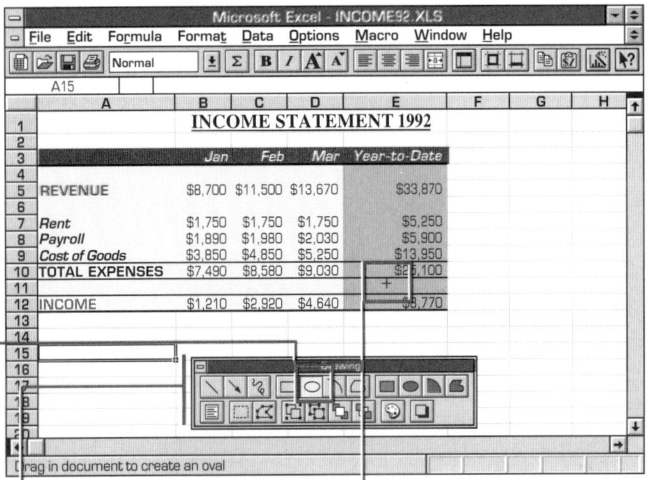

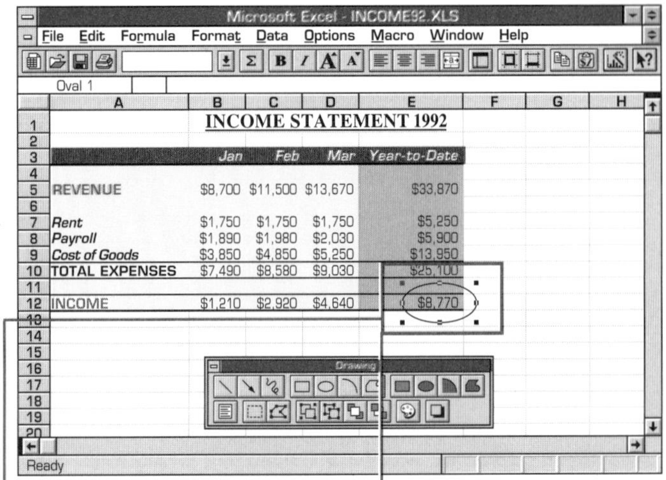

1 Display the **Drawing** toolbar.

Note: To display a toolbar, refer to page 52.

2 Click one of the **Shape** tools (example: to draw an oval shape, click the **Oval** tool). The mouse pointer changes to +.

3 Move the pointer + to the position where you want to begin drawing the object.

4 Click and hold down the left mouse button as you drag the edges of the object to the desired size.

5 Release the button and the object is completed.

Note: When drawing a polygon, anchor each line segment by clicking the left mouse button. Complete the polygon by double clicking the left mouse button.

Draw Lines

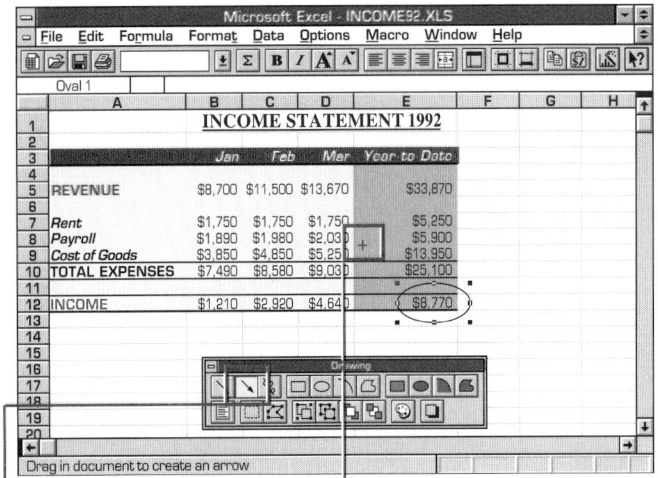

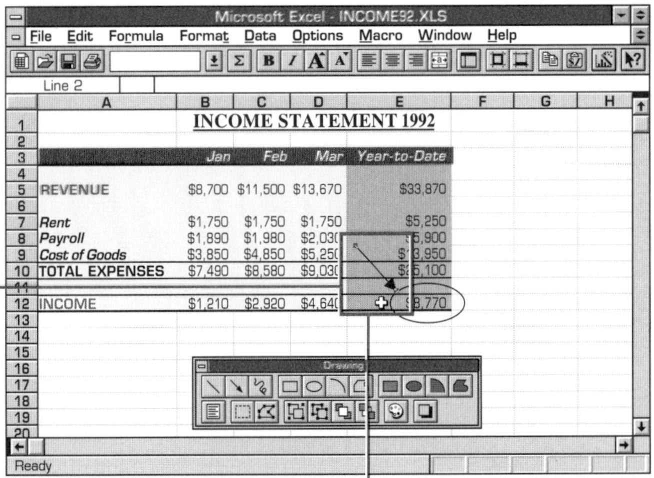

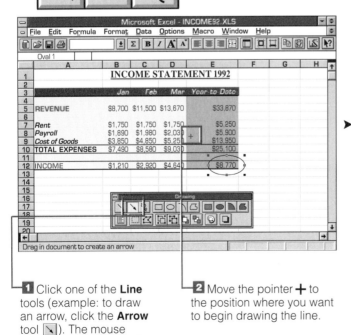

1 Click one of the **Line** tools (example: to draw an arrow, click the **Arrow** tool). The mouse pointer changes to +.

2 Move the pointer + to the position where you want to begin drawing the line.

3 Click and hold down the left mouse button as you drag the line to the desired length.

4 Release the button and the line is completed.

Add Color

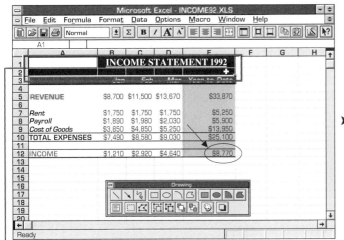

1 Select the cells or object you want to add color to.

Note: To select an object, move the mouse pointer ➕ over one of the object's edges and it changes to ⬚. Click the left mouse button.

2 Click the **Color** tool several times until the desired color appears in the top left corner of the selected cells (example: click the **Color** tool 14 times to display the color shown in the above screen).

3 Click a cell outside the selected cell range (example: **G3**) so you can clearly view the new color.

*Note: If you passed by the color you wanted to choose, don't worry. Continue clicking the **Color** tool and the color will appear again.*

Delete an Object

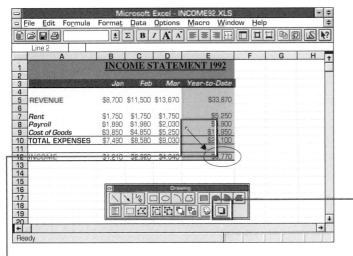

ADD OUTLINE AND DROP SHADOW USING THIS TOOL

1 Select the cells you want to add an outline and drop shadow to.

2 Click the **Drop Shadow** tool ⬚.

1 To select the object you want to delete, move the mouse pointer ➕ over one of the object's edges and it changes to ⬚. Click the left mouse button.

2 Press the **Delete** key.

*Note: For the remainder of this book the **Drawing** toolbar is hidden. To remove a toolbar from the screen, refer to page 52.*

GETTING STARTED

ENTER DATA

ENTER FORMULAS AND FUNCTIONS

MANAGING YOUR FILES

EDIT A WORKSHEET

FORMAT A WORKSHEET

CREATE AND EDIT A CHART

PRINT

OUTLINE A WORKSHEET

CREATE AND USE A DATABASE

The ChartWizard leads you through five steps to create a chart using data from your worksheet.

In this example, the Revenue and Total Expenses for the months of Jan, Feb, and Mar will be charted.

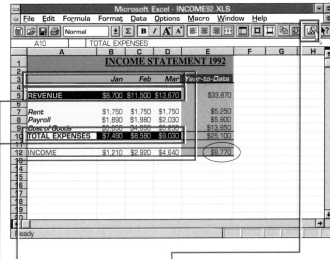

1 Select the column headings you want to chart (example: **A3** to **D3**).

2 Press and hold down the **Ctrl** key as you select the other rows you want to chart (example: **A5** to **D5**, then **A10** to **D10**).

3 Release the mouse button, then the **Ctrl** key.

4 Click the **ChartWizard** tool and the mouse pointer changes to **+**.

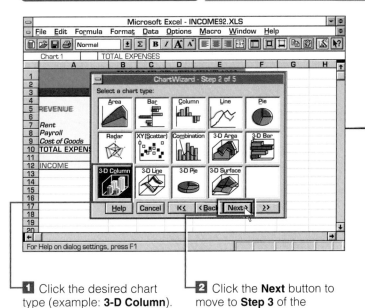

1 Click the desired chart type (example: **3-D Column**).

2 Click the **Next** button to move to **Step 3** of the **ChartWizard**.

CREATE A
CHART

MOVE A
CHART

RESIZE A
CHART

CHANGE
CHART DATA

CHANGE
CHART TYPE
OR FORMAT

ROTATE A
CHART

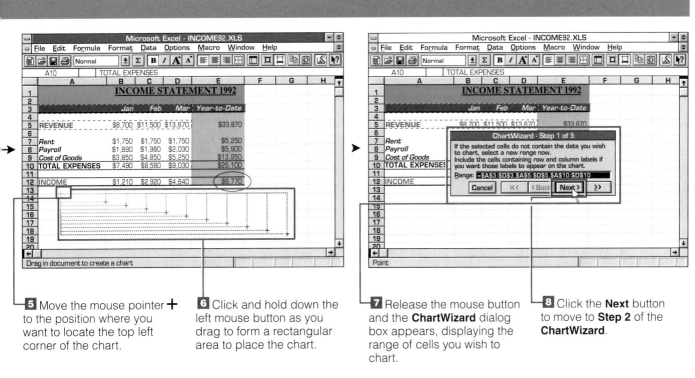

5 Move the mouse pointer **+** to the position where you want to locate the top left corner of the chart.

6 Click and hold down the left mouse button as you drag to form a rectangular area to place the chart.

7 Release the mouse button and the **ChartWizard** dialog box appears, displaying the range of cells you wish to chart.

8 Click the **Next** button to move to **Step 2** of the **ChartWizard**.

Chart Format (Step 3 of 5)

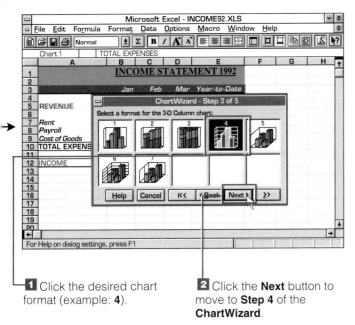

1 Click the desired chart format (example: **4**).

2 Click the **Next** button to move to **Step 4** of the **ChartWizard**.

*Note: For details on Steps **4** and **5** of the **ChartWizard**, refer to page 68.*

CHARTWIZARD BUTTONS

Button	Description
Help	Click this button to display help information.
Cancel	Click this button to cancel the creation of the chart.
|<<	Click this button to return to the first step of the ChartWizard.
< Back	Click this button to return to the previous step.
Next >	Click this button to go to the next step.
>>	Click this button to finish the chart using the choices you have made so far.

GETTING STARTED

ENTER DATA

ENTER FORMULAS AND FUNCTIONS

MANAGING YOUR FILES

EDIT A WORKSHEET

FORMAT A WORKSHEET

CREATE AND EDIT A CHART

PRINT

OUTLINE A WORKSHEET

CREATE AND USE A DATABASE

CREATE A CHART

Plot Data by Rows or by Columns (Step 4 of 5)

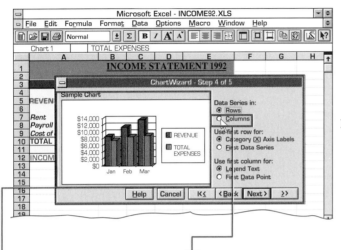

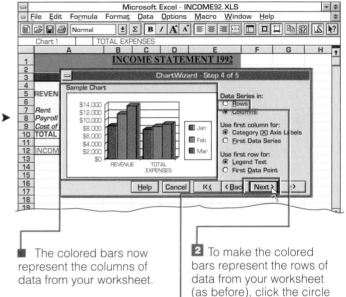

■ A sample of your chart is displayed.

■ Each row you selected on your worksheet to produce this chart is displayed as a different colored bar (example: **REVENUE** is red).

1 To make the colored bars represent the columns of data from your worksheet, instead of the rows, click the circle beside **Columns** and ○ becomes ◉.

■ The colored bars now represent the columns of data from your worksheet.

2 To make the colored bars represent the rows of data from your worksheet (as before), click the circle beside **Rows** and ○ becomes ◉.

3 Click the **Next** button to move to **Step 5** of the **ChartWizard**.

Chart Titles and Legend (Step 5 of 5)

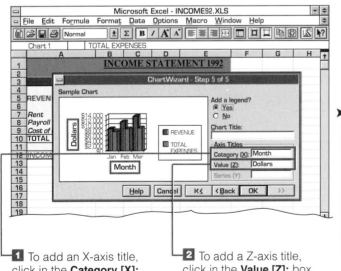

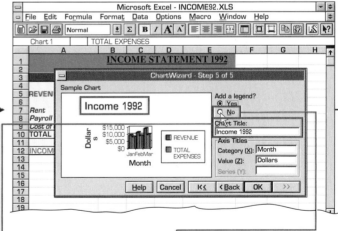

1 To add an X-axis title, click in the **Category [X]:** box. Then type an X-axis title (example: **Month**).

■ The chart displays the X-axis title in the **Sample Chart**.

2 To add a Z-axis title, click in the **Value [Z]:** box. Then type a Z-axis title (example: **Dollars**).

■ The chart displays the Z-axis title in the **Sample Chart**.

3 To add a chart title, click in the **Chart Title:** box. Then type a chart title (example: **Income 1992**).

■ The chart title is displayed in the **Sample Chart**.

■ The legend tells you what each colored bar represents.

4 To remove the legend, click the circle beside **No** and ○ becomes ◉.

IMPORTANT

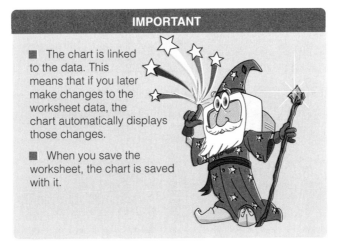

■ The chart is linked to the data. This means that if you later make changes to the worksheet data, the chart automatically displays those changes.

■ When you save the worksheet, the chart is saved with it.

GETTING STARTED

ENTER DATA

ENTER FORMULAS AND FUNCTIONS

MANAGING YOUR FILES

EDIT A WORKSHEET

FORMAT A WORKSHEET

CREATE AND EDIT A CHART

PRINT

OUTLINE A WORKSHEET

CREATE AND USE A DATABASE

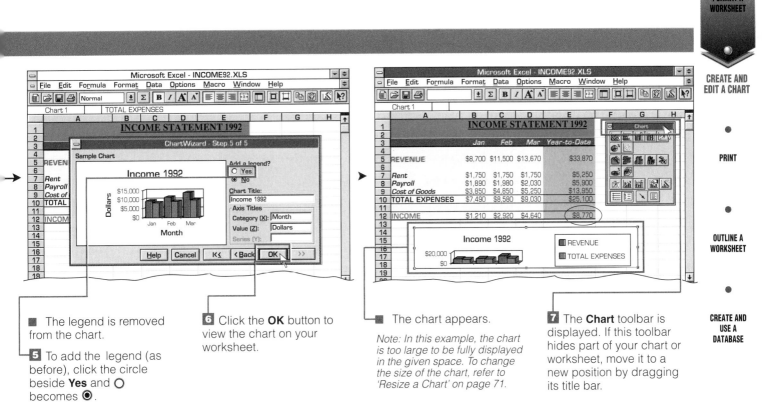

■ The legend is removed from the chart.

5 To add the legend (as before), click the circle beside **Yes** and ○ becomes ◉.

6 Click the **OK** button to view the chart on your worksheet.

■ The chart appears.

Note: In this example, the chart is too large to be fully displayed in the given space. To change the size of the chart, refer to 'Resize a Chart' on page 71.

7 The **Chart** toolbar is displayed. If this toolbar hides part of your chart or worksheet, move it to a new position by dragging its title bar.

Move a Chart

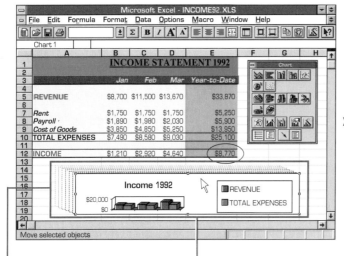

1 To select a chart to be moved, click anywhere inside the chart. Black squares ■ appear around its edges.

2 Click the left mouse button and hold it down as you drag the chart to a new position.

3 Release the mouse button and the chart is moved.

Change Chart Data

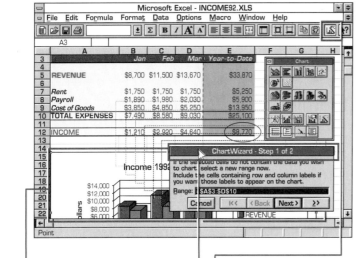

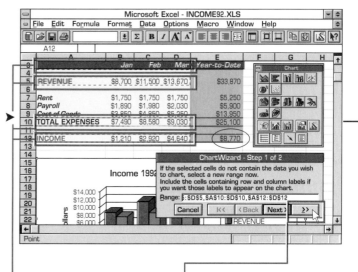

Data from your worksheet can be added to a chart by using the ChartWizard.

1 To select the chart you want to add data to, click anywhere inside the chart.

2 Click the **ChartWizard** tool and the **ChartWizard** dialog box appears.

3 If the **ChartWizard** hides part of your worksheet, move it to a new position by dragging the **ChartWizard** title bar.

4 Select the column headings you want to chart (example: **A3** to **D3**).

5 Press and hold down the **Ctrl** key as you select the other rows you want to chart (example: **A5** to **D5**, then **A10** to **D10**, then **A12** to **D12**).

6 Release the mouse button, then the **Ctrl** key.

7 Click the ⟩⟩ button.

CREATE A CHART

MOVE A CHART

RESIZE A CHART

CHANGE CHART DATA

CHANGE CHART TYPE OR FORMAT

ROTATE A CHART

Resize a Chart

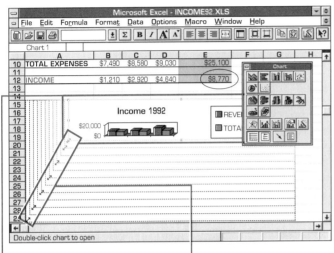

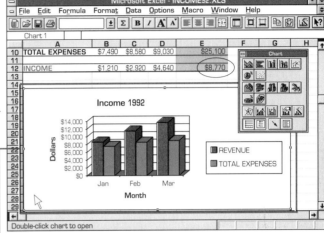

1 To select a chart to be resized, click anywhere inside the chart.

2 Move the mouse pointer over the bottom left corner of the chart box and it changes to ↙ .

3 Click and hold down the left mouse button as you drag the corner of the chart to the desired size.

Note: You can drag any corner of the chart to resize it in different ways.

4 Release the mouse button and the chart is resized.

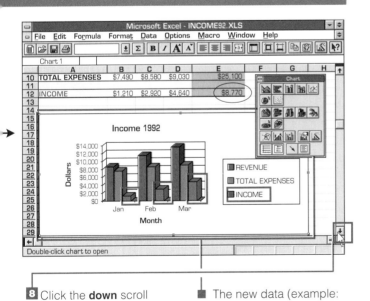

8 Click the **down** scroll arrow to view more of the chart.

■ The new data (example: **INCOME** values) is plotted.

Delete | DELETE A CHART

1 Click anywhere inside the chart to select it.

2 Press the **Delete** key.

*Note: To immediately undo the deletion, click **Edit** to open its menu. Then click **Undo Clear**.*

GETTING STARTED

ENTER DATA

ENTER FORMULAS AND FUNCTIONS

MANAGING YOUR FILES

EDIT A WORKSHEET

FORMAT A WORKSHEET

CREATE AND EDIT A CHART

PRINT

OUTLINE A WORKSHEET

CREATE AND USE A DATABASE

CHANGE CHART TYPE OR FORMAT

Change Chart Type or Format Using the Chart Gallery

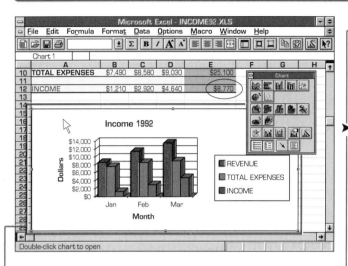

1 Double click anywhere inside the chart to open the chart window.

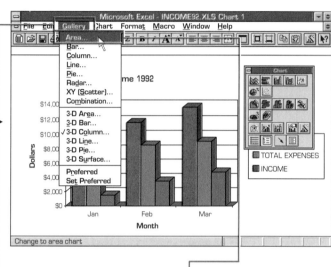

■ The chart window is opened.

2 Click **Gallery** to open its menu.

3 Click the desired chart type (example: **Area**) and the **Chart Gallery** dialog box appears.

Change Chart Type or Format Using the Chart Tools

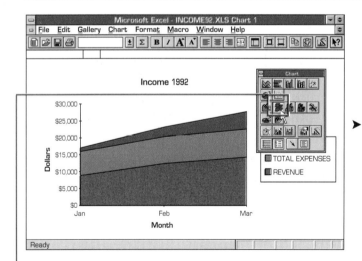

The Charting toolbar offers the most popular formats for each chart type.

1 Click the tool that represents the chart type and format you want to change to (example: ▣).

*Note: If the **Chart** toolbar is not displayed on the screen, it may be hidden. To display the toolbar, refer to page 52.*

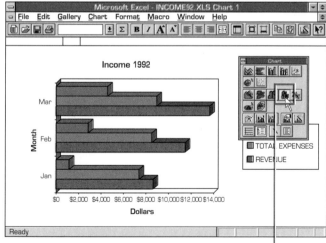

■ The new chart type and format are displayed (example: **3-D Bar Chart**).

2 Click another tool that represents the chart type and format you want to change to (example: ▣).

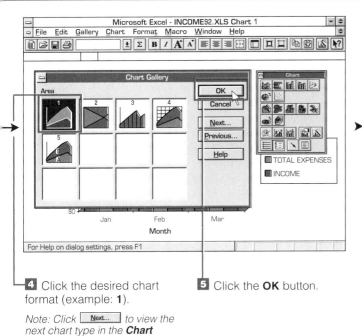

4 Click the desired chart format (example: **1**).

Note: Click Next... *to view the next chart type in the* **Chart Gallery**.

Click Previous... *to view the previous chart type in the* **Chart Gallery**.

5 Click the **OK** button.

■ The new chart type and format are displayed (example: **Simple Area Chart**).

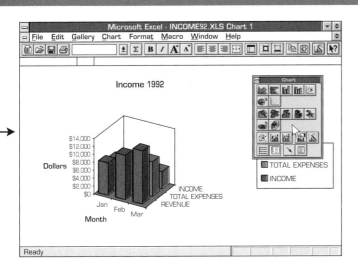

■ The new chart type and format are displayed (example: **3-D Perspective Column Chart**).

You can instantly change the chart type or format by clicking any one of these chart tools.

GETTING STARTED

●

ENTER DATA

●

ENTER FORMULAS AND FUNCTIONS

●

MANAGING YOUR FILES

●

EDIT A WORKSHEET

●

FORMAT A WORKSHEET

●

CREATE AND EDIT A CHART

●

PRINT

●

OUTLINE A WORKSHEET

●

CREATE AND USE A DATABASE

ROTATE A CHART

Rotate a Chart Using the Mouse

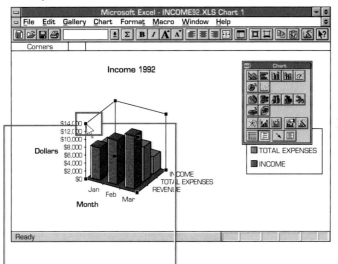

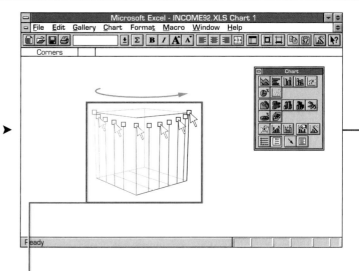

1 Click one of the corners of the chart and black squares ■ appear at each corner of the 3-D chart.

Note: You can only rotate three-dimensional charts.

2 Move the mouse pointer over one of these black squares ■.

3 Click the left mouse button and hold it down as you drag the square, rotating the chart to the desired rotation.

*Note: To view an outline of the chart as you rotate the chart, press and hold down the **Ctrl** key before proceeding with step **3**.*

Rotate a Chart Using the 3-D View Command

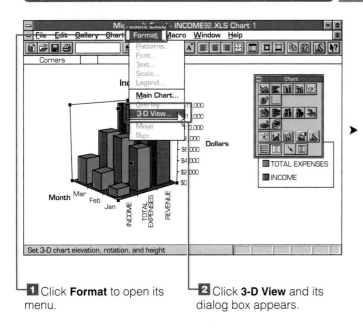

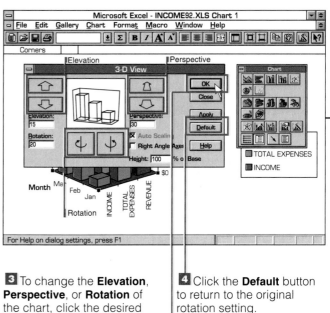

1 Click **Format** to open its menu.

2 Click **3-D View** and its dialog box appears.

3 To change the **Elevation**, **Perspective**, or **Rotation** of the chart, click the desired buttons.

4 Click the **Default** button to return to the original rotation setting.

5 Click the **OK** button.

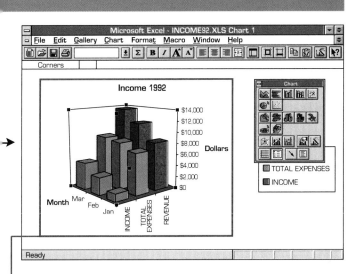

4 Release the mouse button and the rotation is complete.

Note: You can rotate the chart as many times as desired.

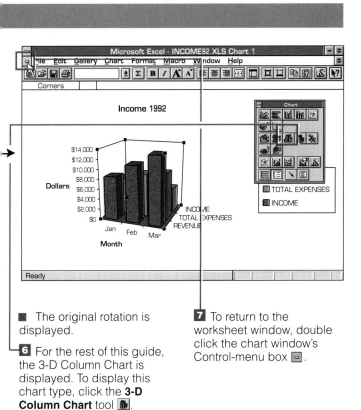

■ The original rotation is displayed.

6 For the rest of this guide, the 3-D Column Chart is displayed. To display this chart type, click the **3-D Column Chart** tool.

7 To return to the worksheet window, double click the chart window's Control-menu box.

ADD OR REMOVE A LEGEND

1 Click anywhere inside the chart to select it.

2 Click the **Legend** tool.

Note: To add the legend, click the Legend tool again.

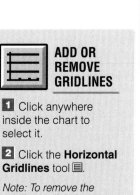

ADD OR REMOVE GRIDLINES

1 Click anywhere inside the chart to select it.

2 Click the **Horizontal Gridlines** tool.

Note: To remove the gridlines, click the Horizontal Gridlines tool again.

GETTING STARTED

●

ENTER DATA

●

ENTER FORMULAS AND FUNCTIONS

●

MANAGING YOUR FILES

●

EDIT A WORKSHEET

●

FORMAT A WORKSHEET

CREATE AND EDIT A CHART

●

PRINT

●

OUTLINE A WORKSHEET

●

CREATE AND USE A DATABASE

CHANGE PAGE SETUP

Display the Page Setup Dialog Box

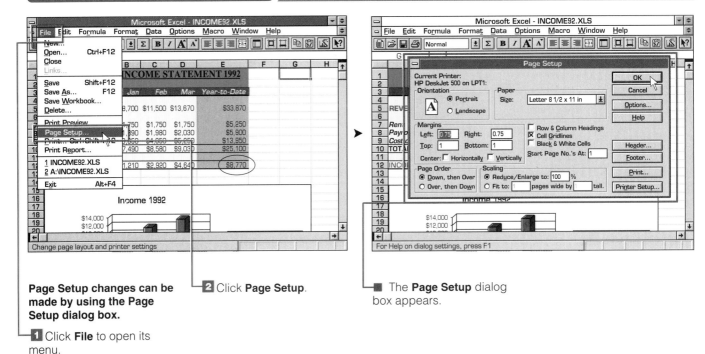

Page Setup changes can be made by using the Page Setup dialog box.

1 Click **File** to open its menu.

2 Click **Page Setup**.

■ The **Page Setup** dialog box appears.

Change Margins

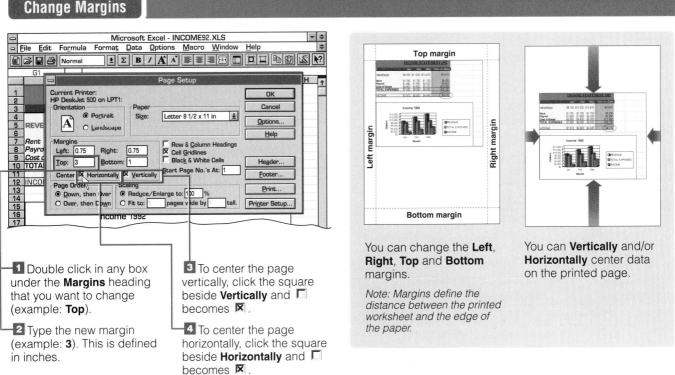

1 Double click in any box under the **Margins** heading that you want to change (example: **Top**).

2 Type the new margin (example: **3**). This is defined in inches.

3 To center the page vertically, click the square beside **Vertically** and □ becomes ☒.

4 To center the page horizontally, click the square beside **Horizontally** and □ becomes ☒.

You can change the **Left**, **Right**, **Top** and **Bottom** margins.

Note: Margins define the distance between the printed worksheet and the edge of the paper.

You can **Vertically** and/or **Horizontally** center data on the printed page.

CHANGE
PAGE SETUP

PREVIEW A
WORKSHEET

PRINT A
WORKSHEET

Print Worksheet Headings, Gridlines and Color

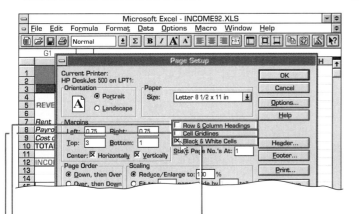

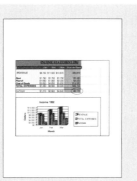

1 To print row and column headings, click the box beside **Row & Column Headings** and ☐ becomes ☒ .

Note: In this example, the row and column headings will not be printed.

2 If you do not want to print the gridlines, click the box beside **Cell Gridlines** and ☒ becomes ☐ .

3 To print the document in black and white, click the box beside **Black & White Cells** and ☐ becomes ☒ .

Note: If a colored worksheet is printed on a black and white printer, it may be difficult to read the printed text. To solve this problem, print the document in black and white.

Change Page Orientation and Starting Page Number

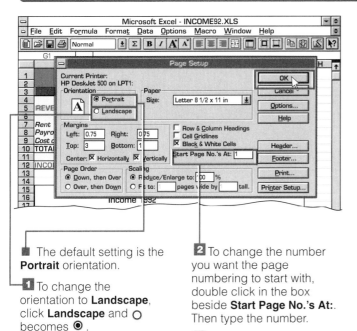

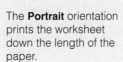

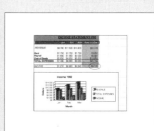

■ The default setting is the **Portrait** orientation.

1 To change the orientation to **Landscape**, click **Landscape** and ○ becomes ● .

*Note: In this example, the worksheet will be printed using the **Portrait** orientation.*

2 To change the number you want the page numbering to start with, double click in the box beside **Start Page No.'s At:**. Then type the number.

3 Click the **OK** button to return to the worksheet.

The **Portrait** orientation prints the worksheet down the length of the paper.

The **Landscape** orientation prints the worksheet across the width of the paper.

GETTING
STARTED

ENTER
DATA

ENTER
FORMULAS
AND FUNCTIONS

MANAGING
YOUR
FILES

EDIT A
WORKSHEET

FORMAT A
WORKSHEET

CREATE AND
EDIT A CHART

PRINT

OUTLINE A
WORKSHEET

CREATE AND
USE A
DATABASE

Preview a Worksheet Before Printing

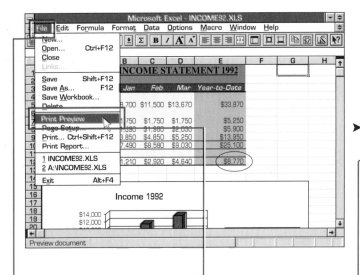

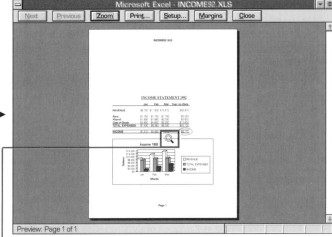

You can see how the worksheet will look on a printed page before you actually print it.

1 Click **File** to open its menu.

2 Click **Print Preview**.

3 Move the mouse pointer over the area of the worksheet you want to view up close and it changes to 🔍 (magnifying glass). Click the left mouse button.

Margins — Change Margins or Column Widths

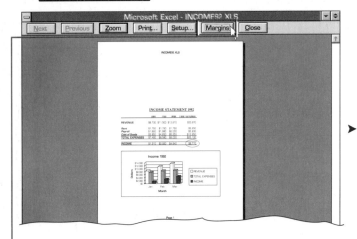

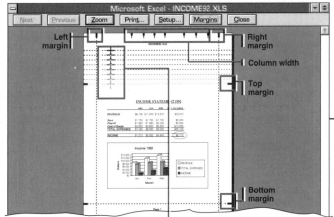

1 To display the current margins and column width settings, click the **Margins** button.

*Note: You can also change margins by using the **Page Setup** dialog box. For more information, refer to page 76.*

■ The current margins and column width settings are displayed.

2 Move the mouse pointer over the margin or column width setting you want to change and 🔍 becomes ✛ or ✛. Click and hold down the left mouse button.

3 Still holding down the button, drag the margin or column width to a new position.

CHANGE
PAGE SETUP

**PREVIEW A
WORKSHEET**

PRINT A
WORKSHEET

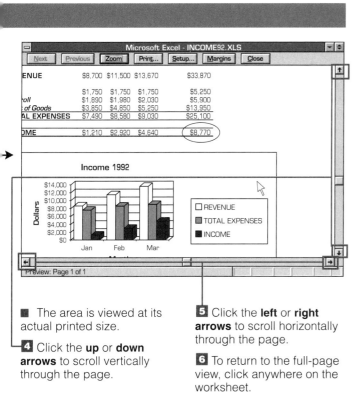

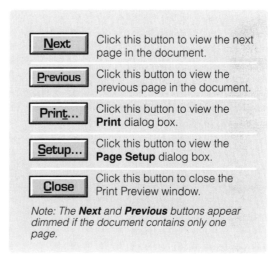

GETTING
STARTED

ENTER
DATA

ENTER
FORMULAS
AND FUNCTIONS

MANAGING
YOUR
FILES

EDIT A
WORKSHEET

FORMAT A
WORKSHEET

CREATE AND
EDIT A CHART

PRINT

OUTLINE A
WORKSHEET

CREATE AND
USE A
DATABASE

Next Click this button to view the next page in the document.

Previous Click this button to view the previous page in the document.

Print... Click this button to view the **Print** dialog box.

Setup... Click this button to view the **Page Setup** dialog box.

Close Click this button to close the Print Preview window.

*Note: The **Next** and **Previous** buttons appear dimmed if the document contains only one page.*

■ The area is viewed at its actual printed size.

4 Click the **up** or **down arrows** to scroll vertically through the page.

5 Click the **left** or **right arrows** to scroll horizontally through the page.

6 To return to the full-page view, click anywhere on the worksheet.

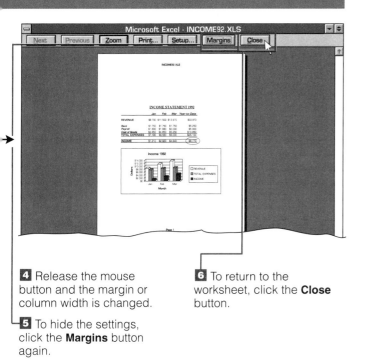

4 Release the mouse button and the margin or column width is changed.

5 To hide the settings, click the **Margins** button again.

6 To return to the worksheet, click the **Close** button.

PRINT A WORKSHEET

Print a Worksheet

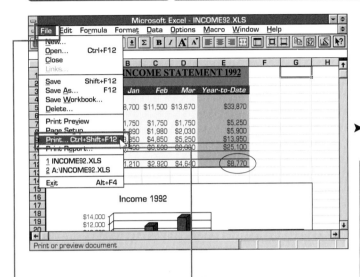

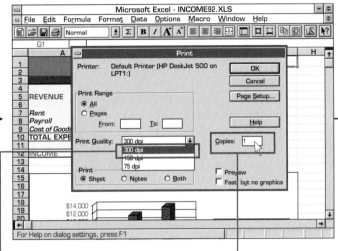

1 Click **File** to open its menu.

2 Click **Print** and the **Print** dialog box appears.

Note: To only print a chart, the chart must be displayed in a chart window. To open a chart window, double click anywhere inside the chart.

Print Quality

■ As the print quality decreases, the printer produces a faster, lower quality image.

3 Click the arrow ☑ beside the **Print Quality:** box and the print quality options for your printer are displayed.

4 Click the desired print quality (example: **300 dpi**).

Note: Other printers may have different print quality options.

Number of Copies

■ The default setting is **1** copy.

5 To print multiple copies, double click in the **Copies:** box. Then type the number of copies you want to print.

PRINT USING THE PRINT TOOL

To quickly print your worksheet using the current settings, click the **Print** tool.

CHANGE
PAGE SETUP

PREVIEW A
WORKSHEET

**PRINT A
WORKSHEET**

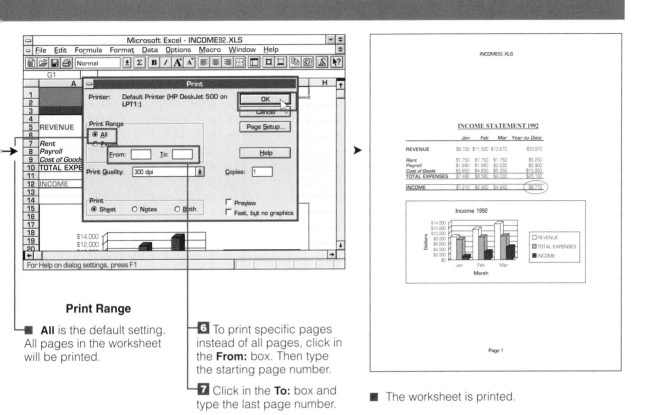

GETTING
STARTED

ENTER
DATA

ENTER
FORMULAS
AND FUNCTIONS

MANAGING
YOUR
FILES

EDIT A
WORKSHEET

FORMAT A
WORKSHEET

CREATE AND
EDIT A CHART

PRINT

OUTLINE A
WORKSHEET

CREATE AND
USE A
DATABASE

Print Range

■ **All** is the default setting. All pages in the worksheet will be printed.

6 To print specific pages instead of all pages, click in the **From:** box. Then type the starting page number.

7 Click in the **To:** box and type the last page number.

8 Click the **OK** button, or press **Enter**.

■ The worksheet is printed.

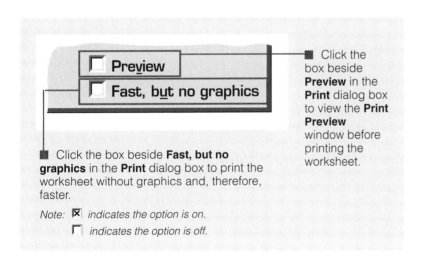

■ Click the box beside **Preview** in the **Print** dialog box to view the **Print Preview** window before printing the worksheet.

■ Click the box beside **Fast, but no graphics** in the **Print** dialog box to print the worksheet without graphics and, therefore, faster.

Note: ☒ *indicates the option is on.*

☐ *indicates the option is off.*

OUTLINE A WORKSHEET

Before Outline

	Jan	Feb	Mar	Year-to-Date
REVENUE	$8,700	$11,500	$13,670	$33,870
Rent	$1,750	$1,750	$1,750	$5,250
Payroll	$1,890	$1,980	$2,030	$5,900
Cost of Goods	$3,850	$4,850	$5,250	$13,950
TOTAL EXPENSES	$7,490	$8,580	$9,030	$25,100
INCOME	$1,210	$2,920	$4,640	$8,770

After Creating and Collapsing an Outline

	Jan	Feb	Mar	Year-to-Date
INCOME	$1,210	$2,920	$4,640	$8,770

Rather than examining every bit of information on the worksheet, you can create an outline to display a summary of all worksheet calculations.

This summary can be viewed at many different levels, depending on the amount of detail you want to see.

Display the Utility Toolbar

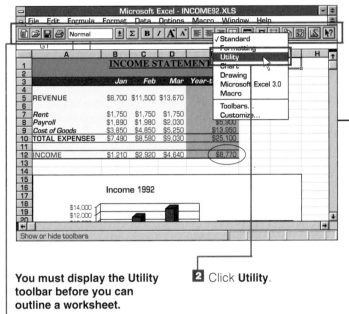

You must display the Utility toolbar before you can outline a worksheet.

1 Move the mouse pointer over the **Standard** toolbar, then click the **right** mouse button.

2 Click **Utility**.

Create an Outline

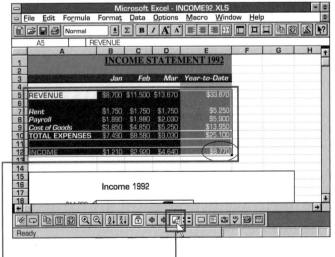

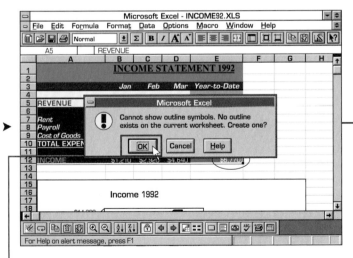

1 Select the cells that contain the data you want to outline.

2 Click the **Show Outline Symbols** tool on the **Utility** toolbar.

3 To create an outline, click the **OK** button.

Note: This dialog box only appears if no previous outline was created for the worksheet.

DISPLAY
THE UTILITY
TOOLBAR

CREATE AN
OUTLINE

COLLAPSE
A LEVEL

EXPAND
A LEVEL

HIDE AN
OUTLINE

GETTING
STARTED

ENTER
DATA

ENTER
FORMULAS
AND FUNCTIONS

MANAGING
YOUR
FILES

EDIT A
WORKSHEET

FORMAT A
WORKSHEET

CREATE AND
EDIT A CHART

PRINT

OUTLINE A
WORKSHEET

CREATE AND
USE A
DATABASE

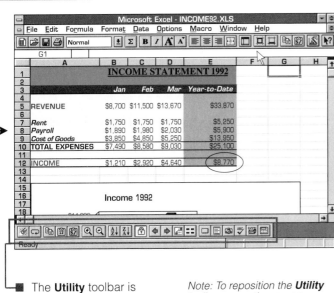

■ The **Utility** toolbar is displayed.

*Note: To reposition the **Utility** toolbar, move the mouse pointer ▷ anywhere over the toolbar, except over an icon. Click and hold down the left mouse button as you drag the toolbar to the new position.*

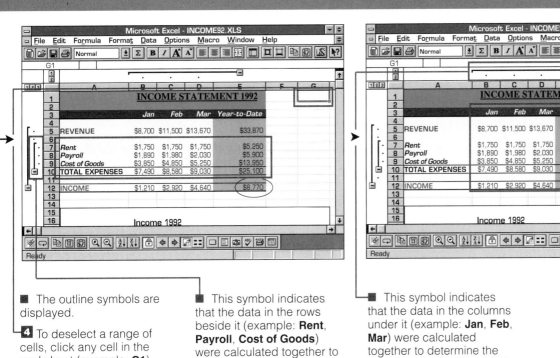

■ The outline symbols are displayed.

4 To deselect a range of cells, click any cell in the worksheet (example: **G1**).

■ This symbol indicates that the data in the rows beside it (example: **Rent**, **Payroll**, **Cost of Goods**) were calculated together to determine the values beside the ⊟ symbol (example: **Total Expenses**).

■ This symbol indicates that the data in the columns under it (example: **Jan**, **Feb**, **Mar**) were calculated together to determine the values under the ⊟ symbol (example: **Year-to-Date**).

Collapse a Level

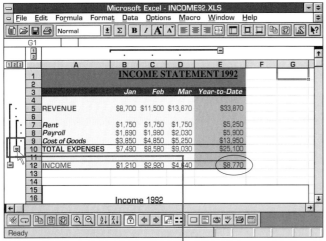

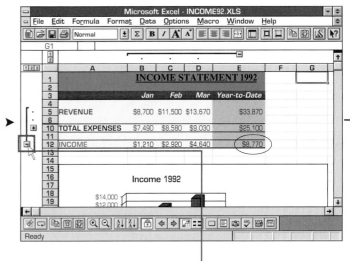

You can hide data by collapsing rows and columns. This makes it easier to view important data in your worksheet.

1 To hide the data used to calculate the values beside the ▬ symbol, click that Collapse symbol ▬.

■ The data is hidden (example: **Rent**, **Payroll** and **Cost of Goods**).

2 Click another Collapse symbol ▬ for the data you want to hide.

Expand a Level

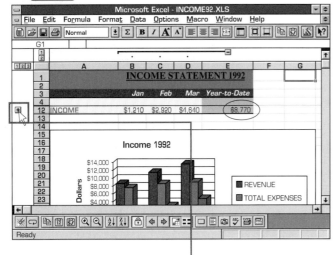

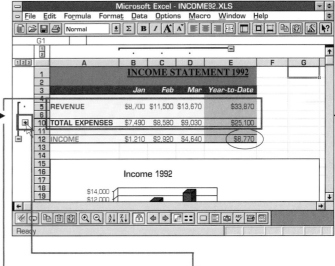

You can display hidden data by expanding rows and columns.

1 To display the data used to calculate the values beside the ✚ symbol, click that Expand symbol ✚.

■ The data is displayed (example: **Revenue** and **Total Expenses**).

2 Click another Expand symbol ✚ for the data you want to display.

DISPLAY
THE UTILITY
TOOLBAR

CREATE AN
OUTLINE

**COLLAPSE
A LEVEL**

**EXPAND
A LEVEL**

**HIDE AN
OUTLINE**

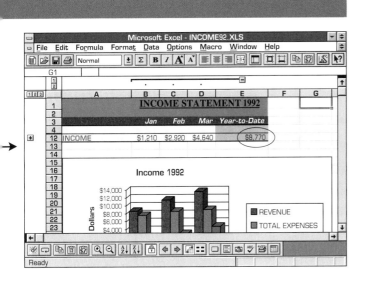

You can also collapse and expand data by clicking one of these symbols.

Click this symbol to display the data for 1 level of information.

Click this symbol to display the data for 2 levels of information.

Click this symbol to display the data for 3 levels of information.

Note: A worksheet can contain up to 8 levels of information.

■ The data is hidden (example: **Revenue** and **Total Expenses**).

Note: You can collapse rows and columns.

Hide an Outline

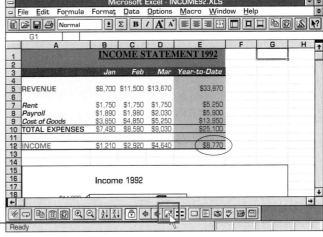

■ The data is displayed (example: **Rent**, **Payroll** and **Cost of Goods**).

1 To hide the outline, click the **Show Outline Symbols** tool.

*Note: To display the outline, click the **Show Outline Symbols** tool again.*

GETTING
STARTED

ENTER
DATA

ENTER
FORMULAS
AND FUNCTIONS

MANAGING
YOUR
FILES

EDIT A
WORKSHEET

FORMAT A
WORKSHEET

CREATE AND
EDIT A CHART

PRINT

OUTLINE A
WORKSHEET

CREATE AND
USE A
DATABASE

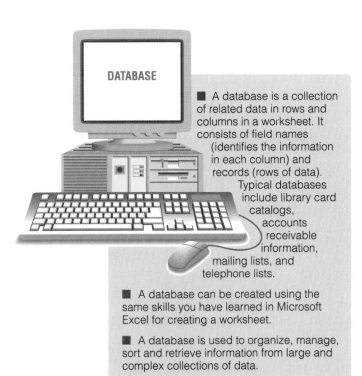

■ A database is a collection of related data in rows and columns in a worksheet. It consists of field names (identifies the information in each column) and records (rows of data). Typical databases include library card catalogs, accounts receivable information, mailing lists, and telephone lists.

■ A database can be created using the same skills you have learned in Microsoft Excel for creating a worksheet.

■ A database is used to organize, manage, sort and retrieve information from large and complex collections of data.

Create a Database

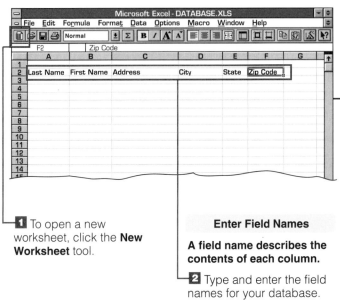

1 To open a new worksheet, click the **New Worksheet** tool.

Enter Field Names

A field name describes the contents of each column.

2 Type and enter the field names for your database.

Sort a Database

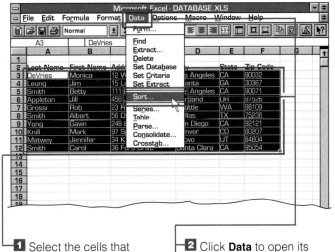

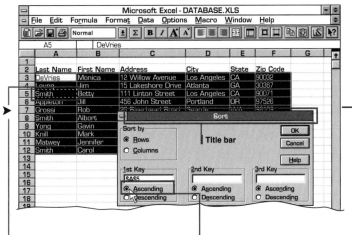

1 Select the cells that contain the data you want to sort.

Note: Do not select the field names, otherwise they will be sorted with the data.

2 Click **Data** to open its menu.

3 Click **Sort**.

Note: Before sorting the database, you may want to save it to retain the presorted order of the data. To save a worksheet, refer to page 34.

4 Select any cell (example: **A5**) in the column you want to base the sort on. This is called the **1st Key**.

*Note: If the **Sort** dialog box covers the database, move the box by dragging its title bar.*

5 Click the circle beside the desired sort order (example: **Ascending**) and ○ becomes ⊙.

Note: Ascending sorts data A through Z, and 0-9. Descending sorts data Z through A, and 9-0.

CREATE A
DATABASE

SORT A
DATABASE

DISPLAY THE
DATA FORM

ADD A
RECORD

FIND A
RECORD

CHANGE A
RECORD

DELETE A
RECORD

EXTRACT
RECORDS

GETTING
STARTED

●

ENTER
DATA

●

ENTER
FORMULAS
AND FUNCTIONS

●

MANAGING
YOUR
FILES

●

EDIT A
WORKSHEET

●

FORMAT A
WORKSHEET

●

CREATE AND
EDIT A CHART

●

PRINT

●

OUTLINE A
WORKSHEET

●

CREATE AND
USE A
DATABASE

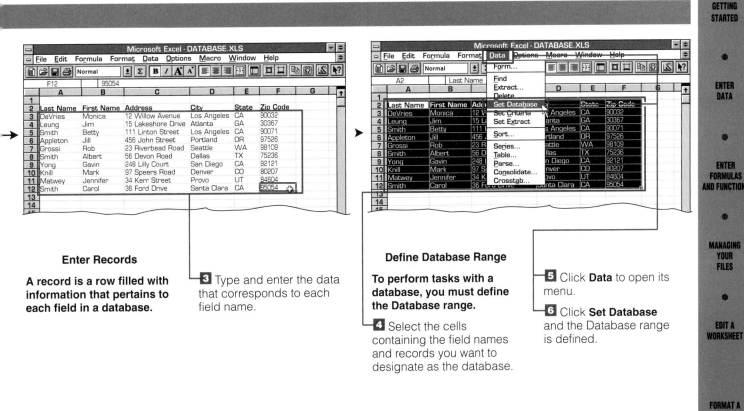

Enter Records

A record is a row filled with information that pertains to each field in a database.

3 Type and enter the data that corresponds to each field name.

Define Database Range

To perform tasks with a database, you must define the Database range.

4 Select the cells containing the field names and records you want to designate as the database.

5 Click **Data** to open its menu.

6 Click **Set Database** and the Database range is defined.

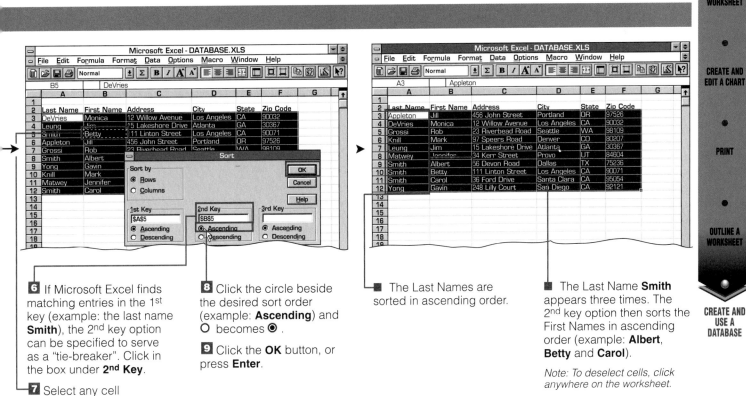

6 If Microsoft Excel finds matching entries in the 1st key (example: the last name **Smith**), the 2nd key option can be specified to serve as a "tie-breaker". Click in the box under **2nd Key**.

7 Select any cell (example: **B5**) in the column you want to serve as a "tie-breaker".

8 Click the circle beside the desired sort order (example: **Ascending**) and O becomes ⊙ .

9 Click the **OK** button, or press **Enter**.

■ The Last Names are sorted in ascending order.

■ The Last Name **Smith** appears three times. The 2nd key option then sorts the First Names in ascending order (example: **Albert**, **Betty** and **Carol**).

Note: To deselect cells, click anywhere on the worksheet.

Display the Data Form

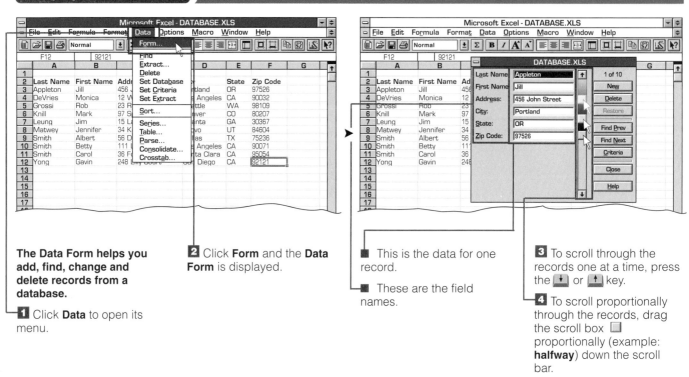

The Data Form helps you add, find, change and delete records from a database.

1 Click **Data** to open its menu.

2 Click **Form** and the **Data Form** is displayed.

■ This is the data for one record.

■ These are the field names.

3 To scroll through the records one at a time, press the ⬇ or ⬆ key.

4 To scroll proportionally through the records, drag the scroll box ▢ proportionally (example: **halfway**) down the scroll bar.

Criteria | Find Prev | Find Next | Find a Record

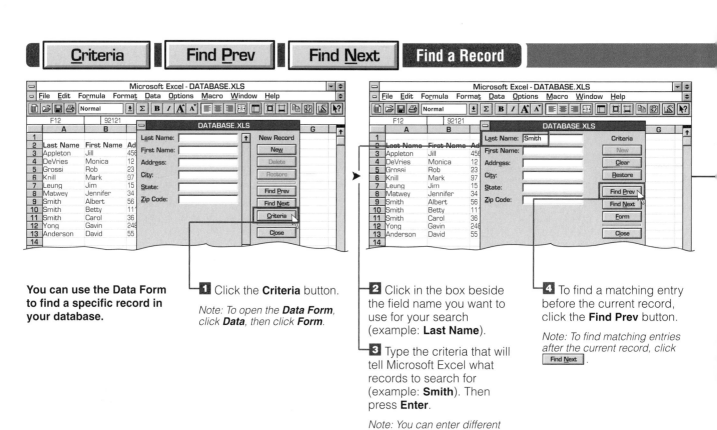

You can use the Data Form to find a specific record in your database.

1 Click the **Criteria** button.

Note: To open the Data Form, click Data, then click Form.

2 Click in the box beside the field name you want to use for your search (example: **Last Name**).

3 Type the criteria that will tell Microsoft Excel what records to search for (example: **Smith**). Then press **Enter**.

Note: You can enter different criteria into as many fields as desired.

4 To find a matching entry before the current record, click the **Find Prev** button.

Note: To find matching entries after the current record, click Find Next .

Add a Record

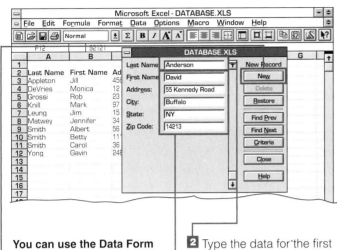

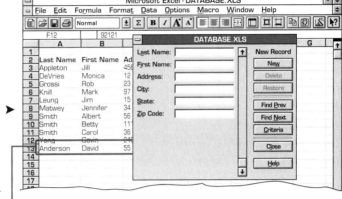

You can use the Data Form to add a record to your database.

1 To add a new record, click the **New** button.

2 Type the data for the first field (example: **Anderson**). Then press **Tab** to move to the next field.

3 Type the remaining data, pressing **Tab** after each field entry.

4 Press **Enter** to add the record to the database.

■ The record is added to the database.

■ The **Data Form** is ready to accept the next record you want to add.

Note: To close the Data Form and return to the worksheet, click [Close].

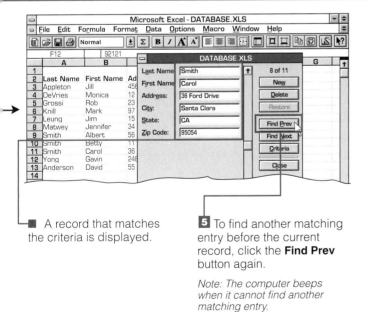

■ A record that matches the criteria is displayed.

5 To find another matching entry before the current record, click the **Find Prev** button again.

Note: The computer beeps when it cannot find another matching entry.

DEFINING THE CRITERIA

Operator Examples:

=	**=10** finds all entries equal to 10
>	**>10** finds all entries greater than 10
<	**<10** finds all entries less than 10
>=	**>=10** finds all entries greater than and equal to 10
<=	**<=10** finds all entries less than and equal to 10
<>	**<>10** finds all entries not equal to 10

Note: These operators can also be used with text.

Wildcard Characters

*	When you use an ***** (asterisk) in a criterion, the ***** is interpreted to mean any number of characters (example: **Jo*** finds all entries starting with Jo).
?	When you use a **?** (question mark) in a criterion, the **?** is interpreted to mean any character in that position (example: **Jo?n** finds Joan and John).

GETTING STARTED

ENTER DATA

ENTER FORMULAS AND FUNCTIONS

MANAGING YOUR FILES

EDIT A WORKSHEET

FORMAT A WORKSHEET

CREATE AND EDIT A CHART

PRINT

OUTLINE A WORKSHEET

CREATE AND USE A DATABASE

Change a Record

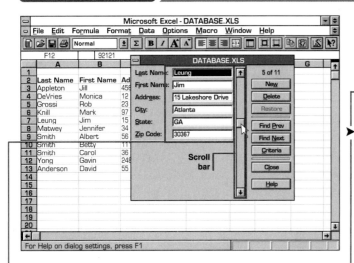

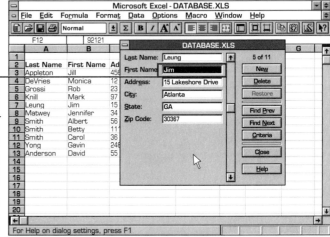

You can use the Data Form to change a record in your database.

1 Use the scroll bar, or press the ▼ or ▲ key until the record you want to change appears.

*Note: To open the **Data Form**, click **Data**, then click **Form**.*

*To quickly display a record you want to change, use the **Find** function. For more information, refer to page 88.*

2 Press **Tab** until the information you want to change is highlighted (example: **First Name**).

Delete   Delete a Record

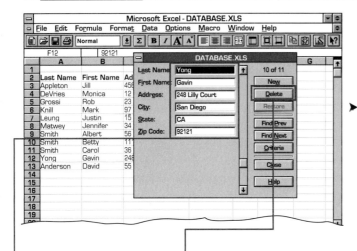

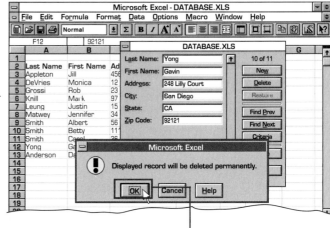

You can use the Data Form to delete a record from your database.

1 Use the scroll bar or press the ▼ or ▲ key to view the record you want to delete.

*Note: To quickly display a record you want to delete, use the **Find** function. For more information, refer to page 88.*

2 Click the **Delete** button.

■ A dialog box appears to confirm the deletion.

3 Click the **OK** button to delete the record.

CREATE A
DATABASE

SORT A
DATABASE

DISPLAY THE
DATA FORM

ADD A
RECORD

FIND A
RECORD

**CHANGE A
RECORD**

**DELETE A
RECORD**

EXTRACT
RECORDS

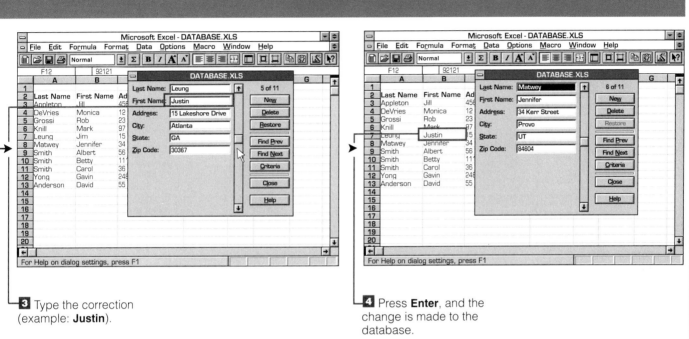

3 Type the correction
(example: **Justin**).

4 Press **Enter**, and the
change is made to the
database.

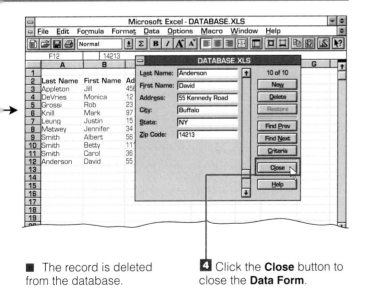

■ The record is deleted
from the database.

4 Click the **Close** button to
close the **Data Form**.

GETTING
STARTED

●

ENTER
DATA

●

ENTER
FORMULAS
AND FUNCTIONS

●

MANAGING
YOUR
FILES

●

EDIT A
WORKSHEET

●

FORMAT A
WORKSHEET

●

CREATE AND
EDIT A CHART

●

PRINT

●

OUTLINE A
WORKSHEET

●

CREATE AND
USE A
DATABASE

EXTRACT RECORDS

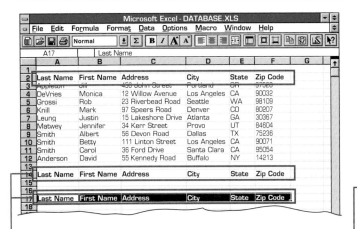

1 Before extracting data, you must copy the field names to two different areas on the worksheet.

Note: To copy data, refer to page 48.

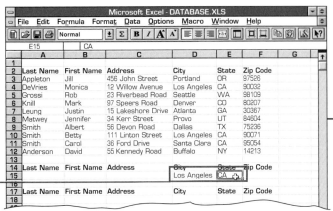

The criteria tells Microsoft Excel what data to search for.

1 Decide what information you want to extract from the database. Then, under the appropriate heading(s), type and enter your criteria.

Note: The criteria in this example will extract all records of persons living in Los Angeles, CA.

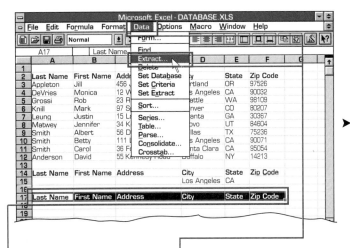

Extracting records involves searching the database for specific records that match the criteria set above.

1 Select the cells that contain the field names where you want to copy the extracted data.

2 Click **Data** to open its menu.

3 Click **Extract**, and the **Extract** dialog box appears.

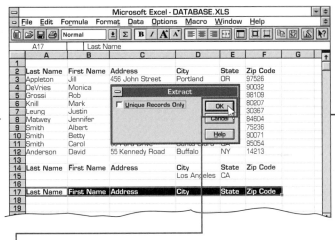

4 Click the **OK** button.

*Note: If you click the box beside **Unique Records Only**, only one copy of each repeated record will be extracted.*

CREATE A
DATABASE

SORT A
DATABASE

DISPLAY THE
DATA FORM

ADD A
RECORD

FIND A
RECORD

CHANGE A
RECORD

DELETE A
RECORD

**EXTRACT
RECORDS**

GETTING
STARTED

ENTER
DATA

ENTER
FORMULAS
AND FUNCTIONS

MANAGING
YOUR
FILES

EDIT A
WORKSHEET

FORMAT A
WORKSHEET

CREATE AND
EDIT A CHART

PRINT

OUTLINE A
WORKSHEET

CREATE AND
USE A
DATABASE

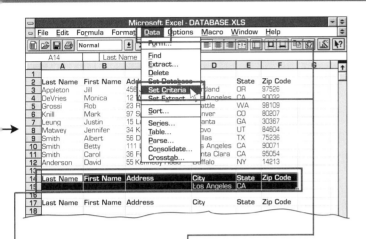

DEFINING THE CRITERIA

Operator Examples:

=	**=10**	finds all entries equal to 10
>	**>10**	finds all entries greater than 10
<	**<10**	finds all entries less than 10
>=	**>=10**	finds all entries greater than and equal to 10
<=	**<=10**	finds all entries less than and equal to 10
<>	**<>10**	finds all entries not equal to 10

Note: These operators can also be used with text.

Wildcard Characters

*	When you use an * (asterisk) in a criterion, the * is interpreted to mean any number of characters (example: **Jo*** finds all entries starting with Jo).
?	When you use a **?** (question mark) in a criterion, the **?** is interpreted to mean any character in that position (example: **Jo?n** finds Joan and John).

Defining the Criteria range tells Microsoft Excel where to find the information for the search.

2 Select the cells containing the field names and the criteria you want to designate as the data needed for the search.

3 Click **Data** to open its menu.

4 Click **Set Criteria** and the Criteria range is defined.

■ The requested data satisfying your criteria is copied to the new location.

Note: This data can be printed and analyzed.

INDEX